programming.architecture

programming.architecture is a simple and concise introduction to the history of computing and computational design, explaining the basics of algorithmic thinking and the use of the computer as a tool for design and architecture. Paul Coates, a pioneer of CAAD, demonstrates algorithmic thinking through projects and student work collated through his years of teaching students of computing and design. The book takes a detailed and practical look at what the techniques and philosophy of coding entail, and gives the reader many 'glimpses under the hood' in the form of code snippets and examples of algorithms.

This is essential reading for student and professional architects and designers interested in how the development of computers has influenced the way we think about, and design for, the built environment.

Paul Coates is Senior Lecturer at the University of East London (UEL). He is also Programme leader of the MSc Architecture: Computing and design programme and Head of CECA (the Centre for Evolutionary Computing in Architecture), a research centre at the School of Architecture and the Visual Arts, UEL.

programming.architecture

PAUL COATES

Routledge
Taylor & Francis Group

LONDON AND NEW YORK

First published 2010
by Routledge
2 Park Square, Milton Park, Abingdon, Oxon OX14 4RN

Simultaneously published in the USA and Canada
by Routledge
270 Madison Avenue, New York, NY 10016, USA

Routledge is an imprint of the Taylor & Francis Group, an informa business

Designed and typeset in Myriad by Alex Lazarou
Printed and bound in Great Britain by TJ International, Ltd, Padstow, Cornwall

British Library Cataloguing in Publication Data
A catalogue record for this book is available from the British Library

Library of Congress Cataloging in Publication Data
Coates, Paul (Paul S.)
The programming of architecture / Paul Coates.
    p. cm.
Includes index.
1. Architectural design—Data processing. 2. Architectural design—Mathematics.
3. Architecture—Philosophy. 4. Computer-aided design. 5. Algorithms. I. Title.
    NA2728.C53 2010
    720.285—dc22
                                                        2009037322

ISBN10: 0-415-45187-6 (hbk)
ISBN10: 0-415-45188-4 (pbk)

ISBN13: 978-0-415-45187-1 (hbk)
ISBN13: 978-0-415-45188-8 (pbk)

Contents

How to read this book

In the main text all references to web resources and other information are referred to by underline.

This indicates that the topic has an entry in the glossary/index which may also include further explanatory information including references and/or URLs to web pages. The index itself is also to be found at:

http://uelceca.net/Index_and_glossary.htm

If your browser is fairly up to date, selecting a word and right clicking it will offer 'search Google for' … which usually links to Wikipedia and may lead to useful searches.

The text is organised into four typeface categories:

1. The main sans serif font for the body of the book.
2. Courier for code snippets which are intended to be syntactically correct text.
3. *Courier Italic for pseudo code which represents the way an algorithm works in the English language, but is not intended to be runnable on a practical computer.*
4. A serif font for the images.

Acknowledgements

Without the encouragement and support of the following people, this book would not have happened:

Work on preparing the text and images of the book
- Simon Kim
- Pablo Miranda
- Tim Ireland
- Ben Doherty
- Christian Derix
- Robert Thum for overall structure

Experiments and simulations
- Christian Derix for attract/repel model
- Pablo Miranda for phototropic robot and Swarm intelligence
- Jennifer Coates for philosophical background and advice on Chomsky
- Helen Jackson and Terry Broughton for work on lsystem/gp evolution
- Bill Hillier for Alpha Syntax and vernacular
- All the students of the MSc Computing and Design/Diploma Unit 6
- Melissa Woolford for organising the nous gallery as the way of exploring developing and promoting the approach to programming architecture in the real world

And generally the nurses, doctors and auxiliaries of the National Health Service, Holly, Bibi, Izzy, Heather and Mounia from BIRU, Whittington. Edgeware Community Hospital and Islington Occupational Therapy.

To Tara

Falling between two stools

A prologue on the nature of architectural research

There is a neat pair of polar opposites to be found in research as it is practised in academe: the two cultures of C. P. Snow – basically 'Science' and 'the Arts'. Since Bertallanffy there has been a third way, which he hoped would unify these polar opposites which he labelled systems theory.

It is the position of this book that architectural research should always fall between whatever polar opposites one cares to define. Building science has hardened into a branch of applied physics, and art history has drifted off via the French philosophers into critical theory, neither of which has any immediate influence on practical designs or designers.

This book explores the kinds of thing that can go in the middle, chiefly geometry and topology, and subsequently the research into generating architecture. I would like to explore this last aspect because it seems that there is a little detail to be put into this topic, and that is the 'new epistemology'. Indeed, the new epistemology is a perfect illustration of how to occupy this difficult middle ground.

We will look at the 'systems view' of space and form. This provides the possibility of modelling space and form as based on very simple algorithms defined as part of a process. The processes we look at are part of a long history of ideas in post-modern thought derived from experimentation in mathematics and computer science, such as Cellular Automata, swarms, reaction diffusion systems and evolutionary algorithms. These new ways of seeing form and spatial organisation all show the phenomenon of 'self-organising morphologies', often referred to by the general rubric of 'emergence'.

This approach seems to provide a nice paradigm for architecture as the emergent outcome of a whole lot of interconnected feedback loops, which replace top-down geometry and the reductionist tradition, with dynamic relations and emergent outcomes not defined in the underlying model. At the same time, this leads to an alternative authorial voice – the illustrated consensus of the swarm for instance – to replace the search for a 'designer'.

The aim of this book is to explain these systems as a first step to using such models to explore how space produces society and society produces space; which came first, the market square or the market? We can contemplate the role of the developing environment as a carrier of information which alters the rules of the builders as they build that environment (the intelligence involved in maze solving is shared between the rat and the maze), and move towards reading architecture as an outcome of a process of occupation.

Algorithms as texts

It is quite common nowadays that people talk about algorithms in quite general ways, which are only vaguely related to the computer science definition. It is perhaps unfortunate that words such as 'process' are bandied about in phrases such as 'design process' or 'building process', as well as being used to describe the mechanics of some piece of software. Generally all that is meant is that the topic can be seen as a set of linked activities. Similarly, to say that the inclusion of time into the description of an activity is evidence of the acceptance of the 'emergent' philosophy often fails to distinguish between any old activity that takes place in a serial manner (the process of building) and the more interesting idea that we will explore here, that, with a parallel dynamic system, you cannot possibly know/predict the outcome without running the algorithm.

So you can play the algorithmic game using diagrams, actions and drawings of all kinds, but there is too close a correspondence between the operations and their description, and the intended outcomes of the process. When algorithms are expressed as text, in some language, then the distance between the description of the algorithm and the intended outcome becomes greater, and, as described below, this abstraction into 'real' language (as opposed to metaphorical 'languages of form', for instance) gives access to the infinite variety of generative grammar. Hence it is argued here that there is a difference which matters between grammars as normally understood and, for instance, 'shape grammars', and that the former, as part of text-based systems of signs, are infinitely more open ended than the latter.

So it is important to point out that algorithms are usually expressed in text. This text is written in a language. All languages have two components:

1. a lexicon of allowable words (or other tokens) based on an agreed alphabet or sign system; and
2. a way of combining those elements legally – the syntax.

There are two kinds of language, natural and artificial.

Natural languages

Natural languages have developed over the last 100,000 years or so and are, of course, based on the way we inhabit the world with other people. Grammarians and linguists have spent several thousand years trying to work out how it functions, and since we still do not know much about the way the brain works (assuming it is the brain we should be looking at), they originally defined the formal structure of language as a kind of artificial set of rules based on Latin (which for all intents and purposes is an artificial language since no society has used it for 1,500 years or so). One of the key aspects of a grammar is the mechanism of parsing, or decomposing a text into its syntactic components. Onions and later Chomsky in the twentieth-century defined parsing systems that were recursively defined, that is, the rule for breaking down the text could be applied to the original utterance, then reapplied to the resulting chunks that were generated from that application of the rules and so on until you come to

the basic phonemes of the utterance. This neat scheme could also be run backwards, starting from the atomic particles of language as it were and combining them legally until you end up with a correct sentence. Chomsky explained this as generative grammar (Chomsky, 1957). Chomsky famously said that a grammar should be able to generate 'all and only all the well-formed sentences in a language'. Well formed here meant syntactically correct. Syntactical correctness does not guarantee semantic usefulness (Chomsky's example is 'colourless green ideas sleep furiously'), but syntactical incorrectness does preclude semantic value – you can't get real information out of ungrammatical utterances, since you cannot be sure what the bit of language is supposed to mean.

The point that Chomsky wanted to make was that, given this generative scheme, it could be shown mathematically that even with a:

> finite lexicon (40–120,000 words for the average educated English speaker);

and a:

> finite syntax (there are a fixed set of rules for combining items of the lexicon),

it is nevertheless possible to generate an infinite number of well-formed sentences in the language: i.e. not just a combinatorial heap of all the ways of putting 49 phonemes together (49 is the total number in English), but an infinite set of structurally correct sentences.

In fact it is easy to show that even the smallest languages, with just a few words and a couple of rules (such as the simple Lindenmayer systems explained in Chapter 3), can generate very large numbers of sentences in the language of form.

Using generative grammars (in Chomsky's terminology) provides a great deal more than just jiggling/juggling the parameters for some design or topic. It allows a much deeper restructuring of the design/idea which allows the widest possible range for generating new designs/ideas. Not only that, but it is using text-based grammars that provide the most flexible and abstract forms of representation if you want to try it with a computer based on the Turing machine.

The advantages of a language are that it is:

1. capable of generating an infinite number of syntactically correct sentences (Chomsky); and
2. it can be *recursively parsed*, allowing encapsulation, multiple branching and large combinatorial possibilities (Onions and Chomsky).

Artificial languages

Natural languages have unknown syntax and the lexicon is subject to at least some natural drift and development. Artificial languages have an explicit syntax and well-defined lexicon.

Using these artificial languages one can define algorithms – one class of algorithms is those written in computer code. Computer code is a very particular kind of text. It is designed to be readable for humans, after suitable training; in this it is much the same as natural languages – no one would expect to be able to read Proust in the original French without learning French beforehand. As Friedrich Kittler, the German Media theorist, points out, code is the only text that can read itself. A famous example of this is the Pascal compiler (Pascal is a well-structured language designed by Niklaus Wirth of ETH in the 1970s, named after Blaise Pascal the seventeenth-century French mathematician and philosopher).

The Pascal compiler was written in Pascal, a high-level language with English-like syntax. To get a computer to actually turn this into executable code – a series of fundamental noughts and ones – we need another piece of software called a compiler to translate the text of the program written in Pascal into machine code. This did not exist, so the first thing the Pascal compiler (remember, written in Pascal) had to do was to compile itself into a compiler! This is known as bootstrapping, and in fact this apparently impossible feat is achieved by having a very small bit of software which starts the job, which is then taken over by the then-to-be created lump of new software, which then takes over the reading and converting process to make a more developed bit of software, which then takes over . . . etc., etc.

What computer languages are not

Many people casually refer to any slightly 'techy' text as computer code, but, for instance, HTML (Hypertext Markup Language – the original basis of the World Wide Web information system) is not a language in the sense I am trying to develop here, but a piece of data. It has a syntax and a lexicon all right, but in order to produce a web page it has to be read by an algorithm written in a programming language, which, using the data renders the page by painting the dots on the screen different colours to make words and pictures.

A list of coordinates is similarly just data. For the text to read itself we need the full set of conditional expressions, control structures and arithmetic operators. HTML and lists of numbers are essentially collections of nouns, a programming text in the sense I mean here also has verbs, adjectives and adverbs.

Computer languages are based on the fundamental operations of the Turing machine, capable of storing and retrieving data and the addresses of data with a set of coded instructions. The reason why the Pascal compiler could compile itself is because the Turing machine does not distinguish between instructions and data (this is the idea of the 'stored program computer'). In a Turing machine a piece of data can also be an instruction, and an instruction can generate a piece of data. This inbuilt reflexivity is what allows computers to bootstrap themselves using code.

So we can write code to generate a reliably (very) large set of algorithms. This is the underlying message of this book, the principle reason why it is presented as a series of essays on the text of generative models of design. The idea is that by concentrating on the text of algorithms we will be able to have a conversation understood by both sides, with common lexicon and syntax, without restricting the universe of discourse to some ill-defined sub-set of design, but be able to contemplate an infinite set of outcomes.

chapter one

Rethinking representation

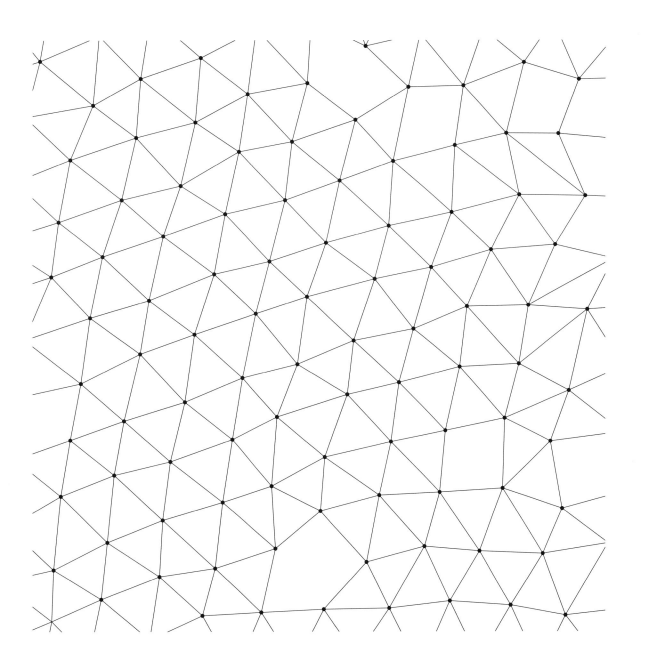

The introduction sets out the initial position of text as design representation. Fundamentally the proposition is that Chomsky's dictum – that finite syntax and lexicon can nevertheless generate an infinite number of useful (well-formed) structures – can be applied to artificial languages, and that texts can be written in those languages to generate architectural objects, taken to mean 'well-formed' configurations of space and form. This is the generative algorithm and the idea is that a generative algorithm is a description of the object just as much as the measurement and analysis of the object, the illustration of the object and the fact of its embodiment in the world.

The position here is that the text we are looking at, being an artificial language, usually depends for its embodiment on some hardware – the engineering product of the Turing machine – and this hardware affords some species of representation, from simple graphics all the way up to programmable hardware, 3D printing and immersive virtual worlds. But this aspect is simply an unfolding of the underlying algorithm, which is still the original representation. It would be possible to orchestrate 300 human beings to obey instructions and so act out the algorithm (like synchronised swimmers) such as in the following.

Some simple texts

As a very first shot, take the example of representing some simple geometric shapes and volumes like the circle, the spheroid and other 3D polyhedra, not using geometry, but small programs written in a dialect of Logo (a venerable Artificial Intelligence (AI) language defined by Seymour Papert, whose history is elaborated in the next section).

Triangles and circles

For the 2D case, this can be verified with a simple experiment using a program with a large number of points in 2D space, initially sprinkled randomly over the plane.

Give each point a rule:

```
'Search through all the other points and
   find the nearest one to yourself.'
'Then move away from this nearest point.'
```

All the points do this simultaneously.

Of course the problem is that, in backing away from your nearest neighbour, you may inadvertently come too close to someone else, but that is ok because then you just turn around and back away from them. Remember that everybody is doing this at the same time.

To demonstrate how this works we can teach these rules to a computer using the NetLogo language which provides a mechanism for setting up parallel computations very simply. The points are described using 'turtles' – little autonomous computer programs, all of whom obey the program set out below:

```
to repel
ask turtles
[
    set closest-turtle min-one-of other
        turtles [distance myself]
    set heading towards closest-turtle
    back 1
]
end
```

To understand this piece of code, first notice that the whole thing is wrapped up in the clause:

```
to repel

    do something

end
```

This is because we are defining how *to do something* for the computer, so here we are setting out how *to repel*. The stuff between the word 'to' and the word 'end' is the actual code. Then comes the phrase '*ask turtles*'. Who, you might ask, is doing this asking? The turtles are the points in space, they are really a lot of tiny abstract computers, and the global overall observer is, in this statement, sending out a message to all the turtles to run the program enclosed in the square brackets [ ], which is the three sentences:

```
1)    set closest-turtle min-one-of other
      turtles [distance myself]
2)    set heading towards closest-turtle
3)    back 1
```

The turtles are being told:

'*Dear turtles, I would like to ask you to look through all the other turtles to find the one whose distance away is at a minimum.*'

Then they must remember which turtle this is by storing its reference in the name '*closest-turtle*'.

Now the turtles are told:

'*Set your heading so that you are pointing towards this "closest-turtle", and back off one step.*'

Interestingly we also have to tell the computer to address the 'other' turtles as in the human language description . If we just asked all the turtles this would include myself (the one doing the ASKing), and we would get a value of zero and try to walk away from ourselves – not a good idea. This is a good example (the first of many) of how we have to SPELL IT OUT for these supremely pedantic machines.

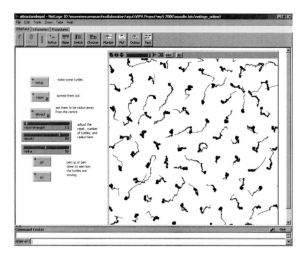

In the top left-hand image, the trails of the turtles are shown moving from the initial random sprinkling to the triangular grid. It takes about 500 steps for the system to settle down, and it can be observed that the turtles quite quickly find a suitable position and then stay there (the trails do not stretch very far, and rarely cross).

These and many other examples of programming in the book are based on NetLogo. This language is a descendant of StarLogo which, in turn, was a parallel implementation of Logo (described in the next chapter), which itself was a development of LISP (see Chapter 3). See Resnick (1994) for a good introduction.

The turtles settle down to a triangular least-effort configuration. See below where the points are linked to show the triangular grid.

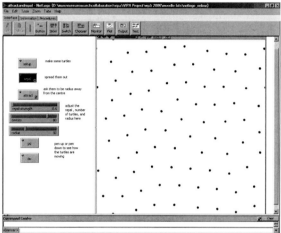

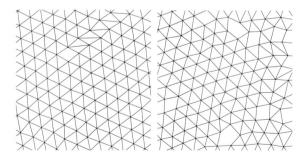

To the left, two versions of the outcome running with links are shown. None of these patterns lasts for long; like all dynamic systems the moment can be captured, but is gone and lost for ever by the ceaseless jiggling of the turtles.

Emergent tessellations

With a suitable repel strength, the points all settle down in a triangular pattern because whenever they diverge from this grid they are in an unstable situation and will always fall back into the triangular lattice. The point to note is that these wiggles are not in the algorithm (all it states is the backing off principle outlined above). What would one expect from such an algorithm? At first sight perhaps just aimless wandering; however, it does in fact settle down as if pulled into alignment by some 'force' not implied by the two lines of code. This is an example of 'emergence' – the idea that the program, by operating continuously in parallel, engenders a higher order observation, which could be characterised as a simple demonstration of the principle that the triangular lattice is the least cost-minimum energy equilibrium point for a 2D tessellation, with each point equidistant to six others. Here also is our first example of an algorithm which possessed epistemic independence of the model (in this case the code of the repel algorithm) from the structural output running the algorithm. In other words the stable triangular tessellation (the structural output of the program) is not explicitly written in the rules; which is an example of distributed representation.

Distributed representation

This is also the first example of many that illustrates the notion of distributed representation. The way the algorithm works is to embed the rules to be *simultaneously followed* in EACH turtle. Each turtle (small autonomous computational entity) is running the little program described above with its own decision making – who is nearest to MYSELF – and behaves independently of the other little computers – I turn THIS WAY and back off. The repel algorithm is the only available description we can find in this system, everything else is just general scheduling events and general start stop for the whole simulation, and this representation is present in EVERY turtle. The turtles can interact with each other and have some limited observational powers, for instance they can 'feel' the nearest turtle and take appropriate action, but they do not know about the triangular tessellation since that can only be observed by the global observer – in this case, the person (you) running the simulation on your computer. This distinction between different levels of observer is a key aspect of distributed representation, and will crop up many times in the following pages. It is vital, with distributed representation models, that there is some feedback present between these little autonomous programs; if each one took no notice of its neighbours then nothing would happen. This is evident in the cellular automata shown next and the canonical 'pondslime algorithm' introduced at the end of this chapter.

It is instructive to compare this bottom-up small program with the conventional recipe for a triangular tessellation. Of course there are many ways of describing how to draw such a pattern by using a simple wallpaper approach.

Wallpaper algorithm

```
Set out a line of dots at a spacing of 1.
Duplicate this line with an offset of 0.5
  in the x direction and the square root
  of 0.75 in the y direction.
Do this as many times as you like.
```

The square root of 0.75 is the height of an equilateral triangle of side 1 derived from Pythagoras (where $height^2 + 0.5^2 = 1^2$; so h = $\sqrt{1-0.25}$), which evaluates to approximately 0.8660254037844386467637231 7075294. This is not a very attractive number and seems to suggest that this algorithm is not capturing the real description of the underlying dynamics, but just mechanically constructing a top-down and rather clumsy measurement of the outcome. This distinction should be remembered when simulations and modelling are discussed elsewhere, as it forms part of the argument in favour of the 'short description' encoded in the generative rule rather than the 'long description' involved in traditional geometry.

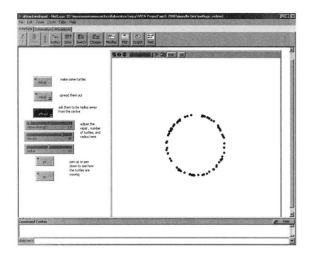 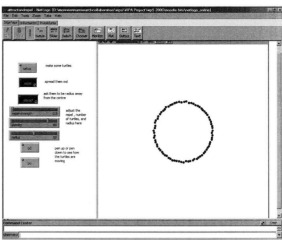

IFELSE is an example of one of the key concepts of any programming language: the ability to get the computer to ask a question about which there are a number of things to process. Known as a 'conditional statement', it has many forms, but in this language, in this situation, we use the phrase 'ifelse'.

This construct example has to decide which of two possible routes to take in the flow of the program.

Cheesy illustration: If standing at a fork in the road, with the possiblity of going left or right, you need some way of evaluating the choices open to you. So there you are, what do you do? It happens you have a note from your aunt in your pocket, you take it out and it says:

> {'when reaching a fork in the road, if it's after lunch turn left, else turn right'}

It is clearly just after lunch, so you take the left turn. Problem resolved. (The left turn takes you to the tea rooms, obviously.)

In the script of *attract* the note from your aunt is asking 'if your distance to the centre is less than radius, then take a step back, otherwise step forwards'.

The general notion of IFELSE is that you ask a question, then on the basis of the TRUTH or otherwise of the statement, you choose between two possibilities:

IF <something is true> **THEN** DOTHIS
> **ELSE** DOTHAT

that is why it is called IFELSE:

formally
ifelse (conditional expression)
> [thing to do if true]
> [thing to do if false]

Extending the model – drawing circles with turtles

The following examples are based on the Papert paradigm of allowing the geometry to emerge from the algorithm rather than being imposed from outside. In this case the geometry is based on the circle, which is then extended to cover more complex geometries such as the Voronoi (emergent tessellation). These are 'illustrations of consensus' because the bit you can see (the two images on the page opposite) is the emergent result of all the components of the system (turtles mostly) finally reaching some agreement about where to be. The phrase begs the question as to what the turtles are being asked to agree about, and what architectural idea might be involved. Generally, the task is to distribute themselves with respect to two conflicting pressures – that of the group based on some higher order pattern, and that of the individual. Papert points out that the equations:

```
Xcirc = originX + Radius cos (angle)
Ycirc = originY + Radius sin (angle)
```

do not capture any useful information about circles, whereas we can write a small program in NetLogo to get one turtle to walk in a circle by telling it to go forward and left a bit (see Chapter 2 for background on Seymor Papert). The program:

```
To circle
   Repeat 36
   Forward 1
   Turn Left 10
End repeat
End circle
```

requires only English and a familiarity with walking.

As Resnick points out in *Turtles, Termites and Traffic Jams* (1994), with parallel computation we can propose another implementation of the circle using not just one turtle, but many of them. The algorithm is based on the characterisation of a circle as being:

An array of points all at the same distance from another common point

To do this with turtles we:

* create a lot of turtles at random;
* get each turtle to turn towards the centre of the circle;

* get each turtle to measure the distance between itself and this centre point;
* if this distance is less than the desired radius, then take a step back (because you are too near);
* if it is greater, then take a step forward (because you are too far away); and
* go on doing this for ever.

This procedure can be written in NetLogo as:

```
to attract
ask turtles
[
   set heading towardsxy 0 0
   ifelse ((distancexy 0 0 ) < radius)
       [bk 1]
       [fd 1]
]
end
```

Notice that nowhere in the procedure is it given where the turtles are to walk to, they just walk back and forth. In fact the 'circle' is only apparent to the human observer, and while we look at it, it shimmers into being rather than being constructed carefully. The result is a ring of turtles defining a circle. In fact there is one more thing to do because just using this process will result in an uneven circle with gaps in as the turtles start off randomly and gather in random spacings around the circumference. How can we get the turtles to spread themselves out? The answer is to do the repel procedure we have already looked at. This version backs off not 1 unit, but a variable amount controlled by a 'slider' on the interface:

```
to repel
ask turtles
[
   set closest-turtle min-one-of other
       turtles [distance myself]
   set heading towards closest-turtle
   bk repel-strength
]
end
```

Illustrations of consensus
A photograph taken while lying on the floor of the Turbine Hall Gallery at the Tate Modern, London, looking up to the mirrored ceiling. It shows how people have arranged themselves in a circular pattern (there is another one forming to the right of the image) without there being any formal 'directive'. The actual geometry is not obvious while walking about the gallery, and only shows up once you lie down on your back and get the God's eye view – when one becomes the external observer. (Thanks to MSc student Stefan Krakhofer for the photograph.)

These two procedures use two references to globally define values which affect the system being simulated, called 'radius' and 'repel strength'. These named values are referred to as <u>variables</u> (because they can contain numbers that vary). In NetLogo you can set the variables through the user interface by using sliders.

You might say that this is not a 'real' circle, but just a messy thing that is a bit circular. But, like the triangular tesselation example, the classical definition of pi as the ratio of the circumference divided by the diameter is famously unresolvable. In fact, the expansion of pi can be used as the basis for generating a random sequence, as it is impossible to predict the next number in the sequence by any means other than continuing to iterate the division sum. In other words, in our universe circles cannot be identified with whole numbers, every measurement of a circular thing is inevitably a compromise, only resolved by its eventual <u>instantiation</u> into an array of bricks, pieces of steel, etc. So repel and attract (which only use simple additions and no funny ratios) seem more fundamental descriptions, generating the funny ratios out of the process rather than squashing them in by force.

These two variables, 'repel' and 'attract' form a useful test bed for experiments. There is a relationship between the values of the variables such that, if you make the radius very small, then you of course make a smaller circle. If you make the repel strength quite large, then, depending on the number of turtles (another variable), the turtles will find it impossible for all of them to comfortably fit on the circumference. The actual result is quite surprising, as it leads to a series of well-formed rings of turtles at ever-increasing distances from the nucleus. In many ways this could be seen as an example of a <u>Bohr</u>'s model of the atom, since the radius is the overall energy of the atom and the repulsion force is the energy level of an electron. (This is intended only as an illustration of the possible explanatory power of these simple models and not a claim to deep physical truth!)

What is undeniable is that, instead of a general fuzzy ring of turtles from the radius outwards, they only inhabit particular rings, which again is not in the model. The text of the algorithm does not include an explicit reference to annular ringyness, but only one circle.

Given the high level of abstraction, we can begin to model more complex shapes and spatial organisations than individual geometric objects without having to do much extra coding, as in the following illustrations. The latter image simply has an additional rule to draw a line between each turtle and its nearest neighbours; see below

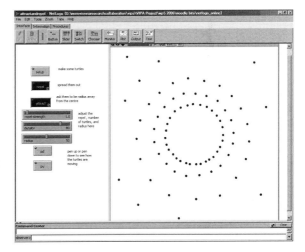

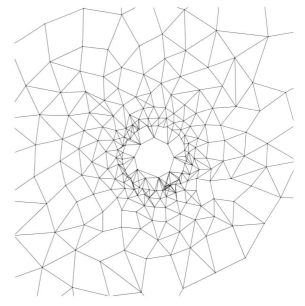

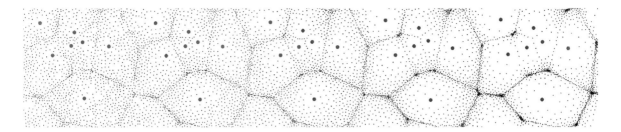

The simulation begins with the two kinds of turtle – 'normal' turtles (little) and 'target' turtles (big) – sprinkled randomly about. Slowly the smaller, normal turtles retreat to the given radius distance in the attract procedure, gathering on the boundaries in ever greater numbers. They cannot go near other targets, but end up in a position which is as far away as possible from all the nearest targets.

If the program models the process to be represented, rather than the graphics of the outcome, it is likely to be a better, shorter model.

This image of mould growing in a coffee cup shows an agglomeration of disc-like elements into a Voronoi-like mat.

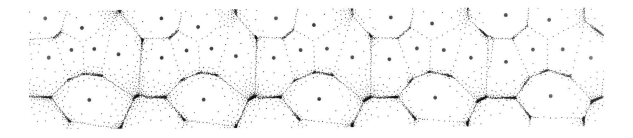

Extending the model – drawing bubbles

A more complex outcome that we can achieve with only small modifications is the emergent Voronoi diagram (dirichelet tessellations). Voronoi diagrams are conventionally calculated using computational geometry. A Voronoi diagram is a pattern which describes the minimal energy pathways between a set of points. Looking at such a diagram we can see that each initial point is separated from its immediate neighbours by being enclosed in a polygon, with each face joining the polygons of all its neighbours.

Taking the two procedures attract and repel, we can make a small modification to the attract one, so that instead of turtles being attracted to the constant location 0 0, they are instead interested in another of the turtles acting as a 'target'. Therefore we can make two kinds of turtle – normal ones and targets. Both the normal turtles and the target turtles obey the repel rule, but the attract rule only applies to normal turtles, who try to stay at a particular radius from the target turtles:

```
to attract
locals [targets]
ask turtles
[
  set targets turtles with [target = true]
  set closest-turtle min-one-of other
      targets [distance myself]
  set heading towards closest-turtle
  ifelse ((distance closest-turtle) <
      radius) [bk 1] [fd 1]
]
end
```

Emergent spatial tessellation of minimal path polygons

In the series above, a very large number of turtles slowly retreat from the stationary targets (larger dots) to form the boundaries of the Voronoi tessellation. This is an example of an emergent self-organised structure, where the algorithm goes with the flow of the problem to be solved, namely draw the equidistant boundaries given the initial distribution of points. The answer emerges naturally from the very simple process described above.

The difference between the code for drawing a circle and the code for drawing a Voronoi diagram using the traditional 'computational geometry' approach is huge: the two trig functions described earlier have to be expanded to many pages of code dealing with complex maths and elaborate sorting and scheduling procedures in order to define the polygons, whereas the step from circle to Voronoi using the attract and repel procedures is simply to have two kinds of turtles and a lot more of them!

All this is intended to illustrate the fundamental point about how representational methods can change when we use the Turing machine to generate form. As we shall see in the next section, the complexity of the emergent forms can be much higher than defining them in purely geometric ways. With these two texts we can represent a huge range of objects, and interestingly the representation hardly has to change at all to accommodate the third dimension.

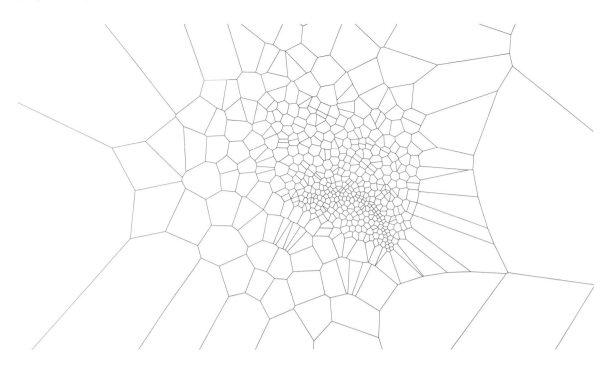

Voronoi by computational geometry – this was generated as part of an experiment in recursive Voronoi diagrams where each generation provides the seed points for the next diagram

The code on this page can be contrasted with the short snippet on page 15. Both are doing essentially the same thing – generating the minimal path tessellation known as a Voronoi diagram. However, the one on page 15 is written in NetLogo as a parallel process of dynamic systems of turtles, the other is written in BASIC as an exercise in computational geometry (code by the author). Not only is the BASIC enormously longer, but it is also much more restrictive in that it does not allow for easy manipulation of the underlying generating points or alterations of the dynamics of the particles. The only advantage this approach has over the emergent version is that the defined polygons are explicitly defined by ordered line segments, whereas the images taken from the agent based examples would need a little post-processing to define them.

BASIC is a very old programming language used in many Windows applications to automate operations. See Chapter 3 for a discussion of the badness of BASIC.

```
Attribute VB_Name =
   "Voronoibits"

'----------------------
  changing datastructure
  to hold indeces into
  originalpoints
'----------------- rather
  than points 11.6.03-----
  -----------------
' defining the cells of the
  voronoi diagram
' working 26 june 03

Const pi = 3.1415926535
Const yspace = 0
Const xspace = 1

Type pointedge
pos As point 'position of
  intersection
Bedge(2) As Integer
  'indeces into boundary
  array where intersection
  occurs
End Type

Type intersectStuff
outnode As point
outnodeid As Integer
  'index into vertex array
  for voronoi cell
```

```
beforeinter As pointedge
afterinter As pointedge
End Type

Const VERYSLOW = 0.7
Type mypoint
x As Double
y As Double
z As Double
spacetype As Integer
kuller As Integer
End Type

Type pair 'to tie the
  triangle nos to the
  sorted angles
value As Double
index As Integer
End Type

Type delaunay
p1 As Integer
p2 As Integer
p3 As Integer
circcentre As mypoint
  'the coordinates of the
  centre of the circle by
  3 pts constructed by
  this point
circrad As Double 'the
  radius of this circle
End Type
```

```
Type cell
item() As Integer
tot As Integer
area As Double
id As Long
spacetype As Integer
jump As Boolean
kuller As Integer
End Type

Public pts As Integer
Public numtriangles As
  Integer
Public originalpoints() As
  mypoint
Public triangles() As
  delaunay
Public cells() As cell
Public neighbour() As cell

Public cyclesmax As Long
Public cycles As Long


Sub voronoi(d As Integer)
ReDim cells(1 To pts) As
  cell
ReDim neighbour(1 To pts)
  As cell
Dim i As Integer, j As
  Integer, k As Integer


For i = 1 To pts
cells(i).spacetype =
  originalpoints(i).
  spacetype ' having been
  set in teatime
cells(i).kuller =
  originalpoints(i).kuller
Next i


cycles = 0
numtriangles = 0
'cyclesmax = pts ^ 3

For i = 1 To pts
For j = i + 1 To pts
For k = j + 1 To pts
' the triangles array is
  populated in the sub
  drawcircle - sorry !!
drawcircle_ifnone_inside
  i, j, k, pts
cycles = cycles + 1
'counterform.count_Click
Next k
Next j
Next i

collectcells (0) 'define
  data for all voronoi
  cells
neighcells (0) 'define
```

```
End Sub
Sub collectcells(d As
  Integer) ' populates
  array cells with lists
  of all the vertex
  incident triangles of a
  point
Dim v As Integer, N As
  Integer, t As Integer

For v = 1 To pts ' go
  through all the original
  points
N = 0
ReDim cells(v).item(1 To
  1)
' drawpoint
  originalpoints(V),
  acGreen, 2
' ThisDrawing.Regen
  acAllViewports

For t = 1 To numtriangles
  'go through all
  triangles
If triangles(t).p1 = v Or
  triangles(t).p2 = v Or
  triangles(t).p3 = v Then
N = N + 1 '' T is
  index into a tri
  sharing a vertex with
  originalcells(V)
ReDim Preserve cells(v).
  item(1 To N)
cells(v).item(N) = t
cells(v).tot = N
End If
Next t
sortbyangle v, cells(v)
Next v
End Sub
Function centre_
  gravity(this As
  delaunay) As mypoint
Dim tx As Double, ty As
  Double, tz As Double
tx = (originalpoints(this.
  p1).x +
  originalpoints(this.
  p2).x +
  originalpoints(this.
  p3).x) / 3
ty = (originalpoints(this.
  p1).y +
  originalpoints(this.
  p2).y +
  originalpoints(this.
  p3).y) / 3
tz = 0
centre_gravity.x = tx
centre_gravity.y = ty
centre_gravity.z = tz

End Function
```

```
Sub sortbyangle(index As
  Integer, this As cell)
Dim angles() As pair, i As
  Integer, O As mypoint,
  CG As mypoint
ReDim angles(1 To this.
  tot) As pair
O = originalpoints(index)
For i = 1 To this.tot
CG = centre_
  gravity(triangles(this.
  item(i)))
angles(i).value =
  getangle(O, CG)
angles(i).index = this.
  item(i)
Next i
bubblesort angles, this.
  tot
For i = 1 To this.tot
this.item(i) = angles(i).
  index
Next i

End Sub
Sub bubblesort(s() As
  pair, N As Integer)
Dim index As Integer,
  c As Integer, swap As
  Integer, temp As pair

Do
swap = False
For c = 1 To N - 1

If s(c).value > s(c +
  1).value Then
temp = s(c)
s(c) = s(c + 1)
s(c + 1) = temp
swap = True
End If

Next c
Loop Until (swap = False)

End Sub
Function getangle(st As
  mypoint, fin As mypoint)
  As Double

Dim q As Integer, head As
  Double, add As Double
Dim xd As Double, yd As
  Double, r As Double
' calculate quadrant
If fin.x > st.x Then
  If fin.y > st.y Then
q = 1
Else
q = 2
End If
Else
If fin.y < st.y Then
q = 3
Else
```

```
q = 4
End If
End If

Select Case q

Case 1
xd = fin.x - st.x
yd = fin.y - st.y
If xd = 0 Then
r = pi / 2
Else
r = yd / xd
End If
add = 0
Case 2
yd = st.y - fin.y
xd = fin.x - st.x
add = 270
If yd = 0 Then
r = pi / 2
Else
r = xd / yd
End If
Case 3
xd = st.x - fin.x
yd = st.y - fin.y
If xd = 0 Then
r = pi / 2
Else
r = yd / xd
End If
add = 180
Case 4
xd = st.x - fin.x
yd = fin.y - st.y
If yd = 0 Then
r = pi / 2
Else
r = xd / yd
End If
add = 90
End Select

If xd = 0 Then
getangle = 90 + add
Else
getangle = ((Atn(r) / pi)
  * 180) + add
End If

End Function
Sub neighcells(d As
  Integer)

Dim v As Integer, N As
  Integer, nbs As Integer,
  cp As Integer

For v = 1 To pts
nbs = 0
  'go through the item
  list for this cell
  (based on vertex V)
For cp = 1 To cells(v).tot
```

```
  - 1 'the indeces into
  array cells
N = matchupcells(cells(v).
  item(cp), cells(v).
  item(cp + 1), v) 'two
  points on the voronoi
  region
If N > 0 Then
nbs = nbs + 1
ReDim Preserve
  neighbour(v).item(1 To
  nbs)

  neighbour(v).item(nbs)
  = N
neighbour(v).tot = nbs
End If
Next cp
Next v
End Sub

Function matchupcells(p1
  As Integer, p2 As
  Integer, current As
  Integer) As Integer

' find a cell (in array
  cells)which shares an
  edge p1 - p2 with this
  cell (current)
Dim m As Integer, v As
  Integer, cp As Integer
matchupcells = 0

For v = 1 To pts
If v <> current Then 'dont
  look at you own list
m = 0

'a voronoi region can only
  share two verteces ( one
  edge) with any other
'but since the edges
  are organised anti
  clockwise, the
  neighbouring cell
'will be going the other
  way. so here we just
  look for two matches
  hope thats ok?
For cp = 1 To cells(v).tot
  'run through vertex list
  for this cell
If cells(v).item(cp) = p1
  Then m = m + 1
If cells(v).item(cp) = p2
  Then m = m + 1
Next cp
If m = 2 Then
matchupcells = v
Exit For 'dont go on
  looking once found a
  match
End If
End If
Next v
```

```
End Function

Sub drawcircle_ifnone_
  inside(i As Integer,
  j As Integer, k As
  Integer, pts As Integer)
Dim testcircle As delaunay

testcircle.p1 = i
testcircle.p2 = j
testcircle.p3 = k
circbythreepts testcircle
If Not inside(testcircle,
  pts) Then
'drawpoint testcircle.
  circcentre, acYellow,
  testcircle.circrad
numtriangles =
  numtriangles + 1
ReDim Preserve triangles(1
  To numtriangles)

  triangles(numtriangles)
  = testcircle
End If

End Sub

Function inside(this
  As delaunay, pts As
  Integer) As Integer
' are there any points
  closer to the centre of
  this circle than the
  radius

inside = False
Dim i As Integer, dd As
  Double, cr As Double
For i = 1 To pts
'ignore points that are on
  this circle
If i <> this.p1 And i <>
  this.p2 And i <> this.
  p3 Then
dd = distance(this.
  circcentre,
  originalpoints(i))
cr = this.circrad
If (dd < cr) Then
inside = True
Exit For
End If
End If
Next i
End Function
Sub circbythreepts(this As
  delaunay)

Dim a As Double, b As
  Double, c As Double, k
  As Double, h As Double,
  r As Double, d As
  Double, e As Double, f
  As Double
Dim pos As mypoint
```

```
Dim k1 As Double, k2 As
  Double, h1 As Double, h2
  As Double

a = originalpoints(this.
  p1).x: b =
  originalpoints(this.
  p1).y
c = originalpoints(this.
  p2).x: d =
  originalpoints(this.
  p2).y
e = originalpoints(this.
  p3).x: f =
  originalpoints(this.
  p3).y

'three points (a,b),
  (c,d), (e,f)
'k = ((a²+b²)(e-c) +
  (c²+d²)(a-e) + (e²+f²)
  (c-a)) / (2(b(e-c)+d(a-
  e)+f(c-a)))
k1 = (((a ^ 2) + (b ^ 2))
  * (e - c)) + (((c ^ 2)
  + (d ^ 2)) * (a - e)) +
  (((e ^ 2) + (f ^ 2)) *
  (c - a))
k2 = (2 * ((b * (e - c))
  + (d * (a - e)) + (f *
  (c - a))))

k = k1 / k2

'h = ((a²+b²)(f-d) +
  (c²+d²)(b-f) + (e²+f²)
  (d-b)) / (2(a(f-d)+c(b-
  f)+e(d-b)))
h1 = (((a ^ 2) + (b ^ 2))
  * (f - d)) + (((c ^ 2)
  + (d ^ 2)) * (b - f)) +
  (((e ^ 2) + (f ^ 2)) *
  (d - b))
h2 = (2 * (((a * (f - d))
  + (c * (b - f)) + (e *
  (d - b)))))
h = h1 / h2

'the circle center is
  (h,k) with radius; r² =
  (a-h)² + (b-k)²
r = Sqr((a - h) ^ 2 + (b -
  k) ^ 2)

pos.x = h: pos.y = k:
  pos.z = 0
''drawpoint pos, acYellow,
  r
this.circcentre = pos
this.circrad = r

End Sub

Sub convert(b As mypoint,
  f As mypoint, start()
  As Double, finish() As

  Double)

start(0) = b.x
start(1) = b.y
start(2) = b.z
finish(0) = f.x
finish(1) = f.y
finish(2) = f.z
End Sub

Function findcenter(pts As
  Integer) As mypoint
Dim xt As Double, yt As
  Double

xt = 0
yt = 0

For i = 1 To pts
xt = xt +
  originalpoints(i).x
yt = yt +
  originalpoints(i).y
Next i

findcenter.x = xt / pts
findcenter.y = yt / pts
findcenter.z = 0

End Function

Sub Draw_Line(b As
  mypoint, f As mypoint, c
  As Integer)
Dim lineobj As AcadLine
Dim mLineObj As AcadMLine
Dim start(0 To 2) As
  Double, finish(0 To 2) As
  Double

convert b, f, start, finish

Set lineobj =
  ThisDrawing.ModelSpace.
  AddLine(start, finish)

lineobj.color = c
lineobj.Layer = "delaunay"
'lineobj.Update

End Sub
Sub drawpoly(this As cell)
Dim tri As delaunay
Dim plineObj As
  AcadLWPolyline
'changed to lw polyline so
  only duets of coords not
  trios
Dim thepoly(0) As
  AcadEntity 'thing to use
  in addregion
Dim boundary As Variant
  'assign with addregion
Dim boundy() As AcadRegion
  'thing you redim
Dim acell As AcadRegion

Dim numtri As Integer,
  thepoints() As Double,
  TPC As Integer
numtri = this.tot * 2 - 1
ReDim thepoints(numtri +
  2) As Double
TPC = 0
' loop through all the
  items getting the
  coordinates of the
  circlcentres that are
' inside the elements of
  the thetriangles array

For i = 1 To this.tot
thepoints(TPC) =
  triangles(this.item(i)).
  circcentre.x
TPC = TPC + 1
thepoints(TPC) =
  triangles(this.item(i)).
  circcentre.y
TPC = TPC + 1
' thepoints(TPC) =
  triangles(this.item(i)).
  circcentre.z
' TPC = TPC + 1
Next i
thepoints(TPC) =
  thepoints(0)
TPC = TPC + 1:
  thepoints(TPC) =
  thepoints(1)
'TPC = TPC + 1:
  thepoints(TPC) =
  thepoints(2)

If TPC > 3 Then
On Error Resume Next
  'got crash on huge poly
Set plineObj =
  ThisDrawing.ModelSpace.A
  ddLightWeightPolyline(th
  epoints)
If plineObj.area > 0 Then

Set acell =
  makeregion(plineObj)

On Error Resume Next
acell.Boolean
  acIntersection, bound
this.area = acell.area
this.id = acell.ObjectID
  'changed to acell
If this.spacetype = 1 Then
acell.color = this.kuller
Else
acell.color = acWhite
End If

' acell.Update
'  ThisDrawing.Regen acAc-
  tiveViewport
makeboundaryregion 0

End If

End If

End Sub

Sub drawcircle(x As
  Variant, y As Variant,
  kuller As Integer, size
  As Integer)
Dim p(2) As Double, circ
  As AcadCircle
p(0) = x: p(1) = y: p(2)
  = 0
Set circ = ThisDrawing.
  ModelSpace.AddCircle(p,
  size)
circ.color = kuller
' circ.Update

End Sub
Function random(bn As
  Double, tn As Double) As
  Double

random = ((tn - bn + 1) *
  Rnd + bn)

End Function

Function distance(startp
  As mypoint, endp As
  mypoint) As Double
Dim xd As Double, yd As
  Double
xd = startp.x - endp.x
yd = startp.y - endp.y
distance = Sqr(xd * xd +
  yd * yd)
End Function

Sub drawpoint(pos As
  mypoint, c As Integer, r
  As Double)
' This example creates a
  point in model space.
Dim circleObj As
  AcadCircle
Dim location(0 To 2) As
  Double
location(0) = pos.x
location(1) = pos.y
location(2) = pos.z
' Create the point
Set circleObj =
  ThisDrawing.ModelSpace.
  AddCircle(location, r)
circleObj.color = c
'ZoomAll
End Sub
```

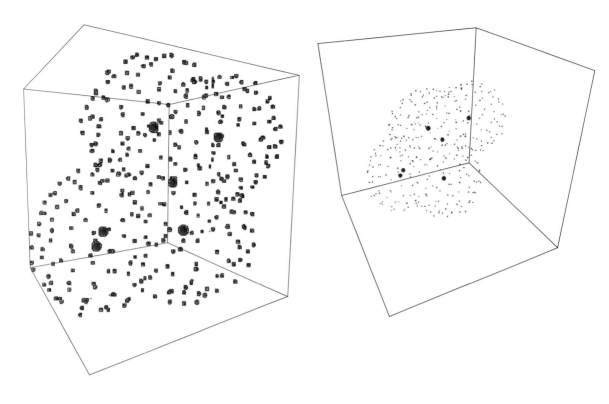

(*above*) From rings of points to spherical clouds
(*below*) Using a link turtle to join the dots

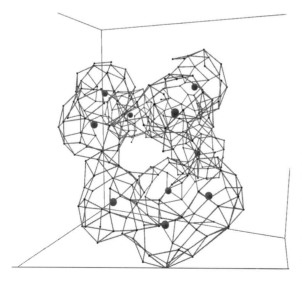

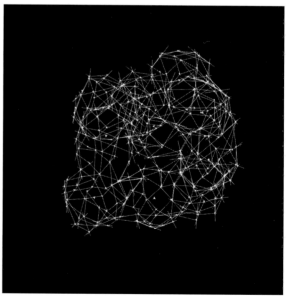

Moving into the third dimension

The code below is pretty much the same as before (there are a few differences due to the 3D version of the language being a revision behind the 2D version, but we can ignore those), apart from that the only difference is the use of the word `pitch` as well as `heading`, which allow the turtles to point towards things in 3D space:

```
to attract
ask nodes
[
    set closest-turtle min-one-of targets
        with other targets [distance
        myself]
    set heading towards-nowrap closest-
        turtle
    set pitch towards-pitch-nowrap
        closest-turtle
    ifelse ((distance closest-turtle) <
        radius) [bk 1] [fd 1]
]
end

to repel-nodes
ask nodes
[
    set closest-turtle min-one-of nodes
        with other nodes [distance myself]
    set heading towards-nowrap closest-
        turtle
    set pitch towards-pitch-nowrap
        closest-turtle
    bk repel-strength
]
end
```

When running these simulations another thing that distinguishes this approach from geometry becomes apparent: rather than in the top-down computational approach, where a lot of works goes on until the 'solution' is presented to you in one fell swoop, here the emergent organisation occurs as a visible process that sometimes has to be teased along with small tweaks of attract and repel values. Sometimes the whole thing descends into a chaotic muddle and cannot be retrieved without stopping and starting again. The algorithm for stitching the turtles together with line-shaped turtles is typical of the bottom-up approach.

Once the closest turtle has been found, we ask each node to create a link with it. The 'link' turtle is a special feature of NetLogo which behaves intelligently in that if the target node is already connected, then this is not attempted again. In the course of a run, the 'nearest turtle' will change so it is necessary to clear out existing links – this is easily accomplished with 'clear-links' (a special button – not shown – is needed for this).

 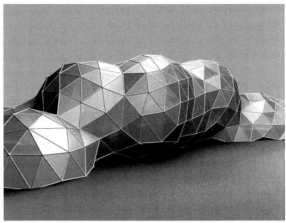

Further processing to develop the emergent
distributions into varieties of forms

  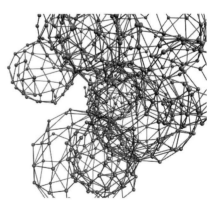

```
ask nodes
[
    set closest-turtle min-one-of other
        nodes [distance  myself]
    set heading towards-nowrap closest-
        turtle
    set pitch towards-pitch-nowrap
        closest-turtle
    bk repel-strength
    create-link-with closest-turtle
]
end
```

One might ask why this simple algorithm does not lead to links which cross the middle of the emerging spheroid, but remember that the attract and repel procedures have a habit of making sure that everyone's nearest neighbour is to be found on the 'shell'. Where several spheroids meet (as in the images on the facing page), a certain amount of negotiation takes place, with things jiggling about until most people are happy. The important point here is that no more code has to be written, this is an emergent outcome of the process provided for free by the dynamics of the system.

After everything has settled down (the 'emergent consensus' proposed at the start of this chapter), the self-organised turtle configurations can be exported to other packages for further processing. In the images shown on the facing page, the turtle coordinates are read into AutoCAD using a small Visual Basic script, and spheres and cylinders are drawn between the points of the nodes and links. Further processing to tile up the mesh and rendering can be achieved with your favourite CAD package.

chapter two

In the beginning was the word

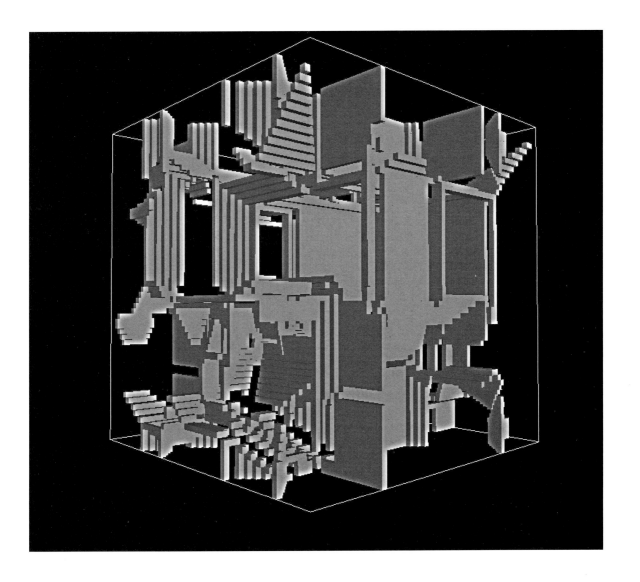

By reiterating the principles of the founding fathers of computing and education, this chapter looks towards a reapplication of the principle notions of how the computer can make a difference in the process of learning, when the computer is used not only as a drafting or modelling tool, but as a 'tool to think with' in the Papertian <u>Constructionist</u> way.

This approach to design leads to an active engagement with the machine. On the one hand, the difference between active and passive use is that of representing architectural designs as code scripts generating emergent outcomes, and on the other hand representing them as static geometry.

The early pioneers of <u>artificial intelligence</u> at the Massachusetts Institute of Technology (MIT) began to think about the epistemological importance of their new machine – the computer – almost as soon as it was invented. It was realised that the computer allowed a new way of thinking about knowledge, and was not just a more powerful calculator or data processor. This led to seeing computers as creative tools for learning. The original motivation of the pioneers could perhaps be summarised as: the need to encourage abstract thought rather than learn the standard procedures, and the aspect of the unexplored side of computer literacy, that it is not only necessary to be able to read the new media, but also to write them too. The interesting thing about the early work was the focus on language and how best to define and implement the artificial languages that were needed to explore the computer's abilities.

<u>Marvin Minsky</u> put it very well when he asserted that:

> 'you have to distinguish between writing a program that helps you to test your theory or analyse your results, and writing a program that is your theory'.

Thus the primary assertion of this book is flagged up, but here we are perhaps modifying the statement to replace the word 'theory' with 'design':

> 'you have to distinguish between writing a program that helps you to test your design or analyse your results, and writing a program that *is* your design'.

One might imagine that there are a huge number of differences between the current situation and that of the late 1960s in both design and computers, hardware and software, and the status of architecture itself as a practice. In fact, as this chapter hopes to uncover, very little has changed in the last 40 years in terms of the aims and intentions of people designing computer systems (including the state of mind of the author it has to be said), and in fact we seem to have forgotten large chunks of stuff which we would do well to remember.

By reiterating the principles of the founding fathers of computing and education, I hope to work towards a reapplication of the principle notions of what difference a computer makes, and how the early pioneers still have many useful things to say in the context of 3D design.

Seymour Papert

Seymour Papert was, with Marvin Minsky, one of the people in at the birth of the MIT artificial intelligence (AI) project in the late 1950s. It was a mixture of computing science, philosophy and mathematics that initially gave birth to LISP, an elegant formalism of an artificial language upon whose foundations many other languages and projects were based. For the most part, AI was making the assumption that intelligence was best seen as the application of formal systems of logic, such as first order predicate calculus. This emphasis on well-defined syntactically consistent artificial languages is a leitmotif in the writings of Papert and others (especially McCarthy, of course, who developed the language). Chomsky (*Syntactic Structures,* 1957), who showed how to define a human language as a recursively defined structure of functions, gave an impetus to the development of LISP, and it was certainly seen as a conceptual leap above BASIC, FORTRAN and all the engineering-based languages, which were ill-structured, inconsistent and clumsy. Papert reserves many words of abuse for BASIC when talking about using computers to teach children. Not only that, but it has been a commonplace view among programmers that BASIC is bad for your brain. A classic example of this (among programmers) is Dijkstra's note 'GO TO statement considered Harmful' (1968). This was published in *Communications of the Association for Computing Machinery,* founded in 1947, which August Body is the grandfather of all such organisations. This point is taken up by Kay (see page 29).

Papert, however, also worked with Piaget (1896–1980) in the 1960s at his 'International centre for genetic epistemology' (1955–80), and it is this experience which he credits for turning him towards the study of learning and the development of strategies for learning – 'making children into epistemologists', as he says.

For Papert, Piaget introduced the distinction between concrete thinking and formal thinking, between learning and teaching. Piaget insisted in the Geneva Institute that we should see children as 'builders of their own intellectual structures'. Papert insists that the computer can concretise the formal. So that it is not that 'the computer programs the child', but that 'the child programs the computer'. (This and all following quotes are taken from his canonical book *Mindstorms* (Papert, 1980), published in the year of Piaget's death.) Papert begins the book by stating:

> Two major themes – that children can learn to use computers in a masterful way, and that learning to use computers can change the way we learn everything else – have shaped my research agenda on computers and education.

In his development of the turtle/computer as an object to think with, Papert describes it as:

> an object in which there is an intersection of cultural presence, embedded knowledge and the possibility for personal identification'

Thus bridges can be made between the turtle geometry and the body geometry of the child. Added to this was the aim of providing an environment where the learner is 'embedded in a learning environment as one is as an infant learning to speak'. The computer, if sufficiently flexible and friendly, could provide this environment, and 'as in a good art class the child is learning technical knowledge as a means to get to a creative and personally defined end'. This is summed up by his assertion that 'there will be a product'.

Papert is, of course, mostly talking about new approaches to making children understand the fundamentals of maths and geometry, but it is an easy jump to architecture. There are many overlaps between the project of Papert and Kay and the aims of this book, at least in the development of an understanding of the computer in the simulation and generation of spatial patterns. Papert's assertion that 'our culture is relatively poor in models of systematic procedures, there is no word for nested loops or bug or debugging' may seem irrelevant in the architectural context, but it is often illuminating for students to look again at the age old conundrums of space and spatial organisation using a somewhat recalcitrant (but always listening) computer

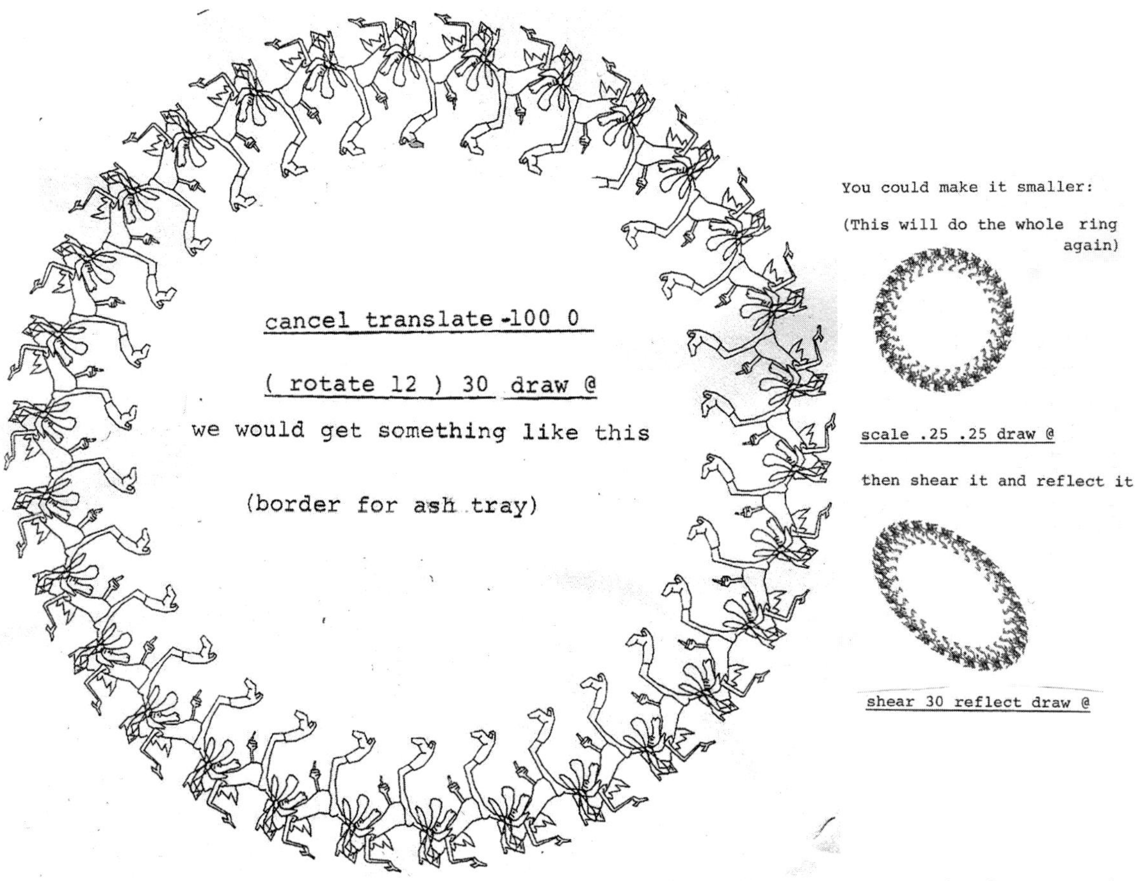

cancel translate -100 0

(rotate 12) 30 draw @

we would get something like this

(border for ash tray)

You could make it smaller:

(This will do the whole ring again)

scale .25 .25 draw @

then shear it and reflect it

shear 30 reflect draw @

Freewheelin Franklin Ashtray – image taken from a tutorial handout for the 'shape processor' (Coates and Frazer Eurographics, 1982) for first-year students at Liverpool polytechnic by the author. The scripting language allowed the manipulation of digitised shapes with a simple LISP-like syntax to allow the development of subsequent versions. (Freewheelin Franklin is a cartoon character by Robert Crumb.)

to tease out the convolutions in some idea about space and form.

He is particularly keen on pointing out that Logo hides the mechanics (the plumbing) of the interaction with the computer. In Papert's case this is described by comparing Logo with BASIC, which he describes as engineering-based, unsophisticated and only originally justifiable with reference to the tiny memories of the original educational computers ('there will soon be machines more powerful than the Tandy radio shack computer'), a fervent hope that we all shared in 1979, and that came true eventually.

'Logo is more powerful, more general and more intelligible', he finally asserts. As an example of this, consider the idea of recursion. First of all, why should an architectural student want to explore this technique? Partly it is because it provides a way of thinking about more subtle and interesting things than the simple LOOP; it encapsulates the ideas of self-similarity and yet difference across scales, it simplifies and explains seemingly complex objects, it is a clear way to thinking about many branching and subdivision type systems which are often needed in architecture. The idea that something should be made out of just itself is an odd one, and hard to grasp. There seems to be something missing, the idea lacks the 'subject > object' relation of the observable world. Using a recursively defined language like LISP or Logo, where a function can be arranged to call itself as its own argument, is a clear demonstration that it is both possible and easy. The mechanics are set out and, 'lo', a cauliflower emerges!

Once this has been observed and digested, the student can go on to modify the code and try to match the mechanics to the architectural problem at hand. This contrasts with the imposition of arbitrary geometrical patterns onto an architectural idea where the actual structure of the generator is unexplored and unmatched in any way to the problem at hand. In other words, not taking part in the problem exploration process of the student, but just one of a library of ready-made images.

Another advantage of working this way is that designers are encouraged to be explicit about their intentions, and then translate these intentions into algorithmic relations, producing a multiplicity of relevant, but often counter-intuitive outcomes, which challenge their learnt preconceptions.

Alan Kay

Papert himself recognised Kay as one of the people he saw as working towards his own goals. Throughout the 1970s at the Xerox Research Institute and also at MIT, and latterly Apple computers, Kay worked constantly to design a machine that would create the interactive self-learning experience that Papert was also looking for. Essentially Kay was a computer nerd and a programmer, and his essay *The Early History of Smalltalk* (Kay, 1993) is a fundamental look at the way the design of a language can derive from a philosophy of education. Kay is more up for a good nerdy quote than Papert. In the *New Media Reader*'s (Wardrip and Bruin, 2003) collection of essays, Kay's 'personal dynamic media' is introduced with a reference to Papert, followed by his remark:

> I was possessed by the analogy between print literacy and Logo. While designing the FLEX machine I had believed that end users needed to be able to program before the computer could become truly theirs – but here was a real demonstration, and with children! The ability to 'read' a medium means you can access materials and tools generated by others. The ability to 'write' in a medium means you can generate materials and tools for others. You must have both to be literate. In print writing, the tools you generate are rhetorical; they demonstrate and convince. In computer writing, the tools you generate are processes; they simulate and decide.
>
> Smalltalk was part of this larger pursuit of ARPA, and later of Xerox PARC, that I called personal computing. There were so many people involved in each stage from the research communities that the accurate allocation of credit for ideas is intractably difficult. Instead, as Bob Barton liked to quote Goethe, we should 'share in the excitement of discovery without vain attempts to claim priority'.
>
> ('User Interface: A Personal View', 193)

In his categorisation of programming languages, Kay shares Papert's scorn for BASIC *et al.*:

> Programming languages can be categorized in a number of ways: imperative, applicative, logic-based, problem-oriented, etc. But they all seem to be either an 'agglutination of features' or a 'crystallization of style'. COBOL, PL/1, AdA, etc., belong to the first kind; LISP, APL – and Smalltalk – are the second kind.

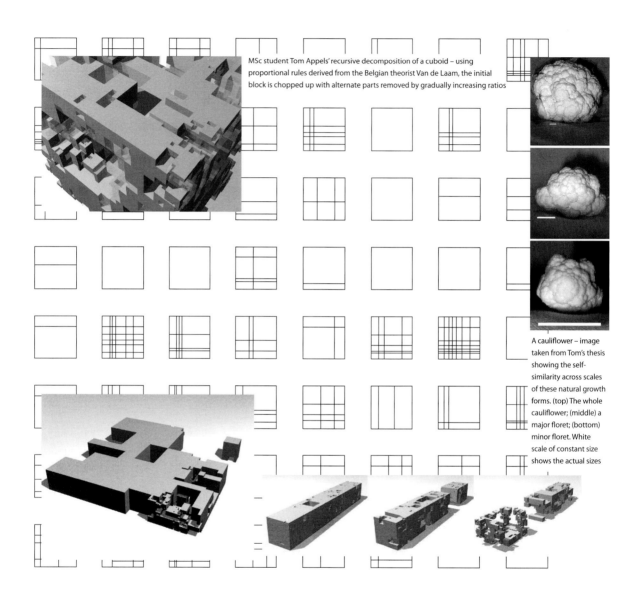

MSc student Tom Appels' recursive decomposition of a cuboid – using proportional rules derived from the Belgian theorist Van de Laam, the initial block is chopped up with alternate parts removed by gradually increasing ratios

A cauliflower – image taken from Tom's thesis showing the self-similarity across scales of these natural growth forms. (top) The whole cauliflower; (middle) a major floret; (bottom) minor floret. White scale of constant size shows the actual sizes

It is probably not an accident that the agglutinative languages all seem to have been instigated by committees, and the crystallization languages by a single person.

The distinction between the committee language and the personal creation is quite nice, but the author prefers to see this as a distinction between a computer language as an engineering project (FORTRAN, BASIC, etc) and as a linguistic one. There are a number of telling passages in the *History of LISP* (McCarthy, 1978) where McCarthy is clearly showing that the overall syntax of the language was defined before the detailed implementation details were worked out, especially the way variables were returned on the fly from evaluated functions, how the memory was to be organised and so on. What mattered was the clean syntax, that consistency was all (if you could do it to a variable, then you could do it to a function, a list anything . . .). This makes it possible to 'guess' what the correct syntax should be for an unfamiliar construction, unlike FORTRAN whose early manuals used to be described as 'a list of known bugs' by cynical programmers in the 1960s.

There were some exceptions to this all encompassing elegance, in particular the author finds it particularly comforting to read:

> . . . and it seemed natural to use the lamda-notation of Church (1941). I didn't understand the rest of his book, so I wasn't tempted to try to implement his more general mechanism for defining functions. Church used higher order functionals instead of using conditional expressions. Conditional expressions are much more readily implemented on computers.
>
> (McCarthy, 1978)

Kay begins his history of 'Object Oriented Programming' (a term now widely used that he invented 30 years ago) as follows:

> I 'barely saw' the idea … in 1961 while a programmer in the air force The first was on the Burroghs 223 in the form of a style for transporting files from one air training command installation to another. There were no standard operating systems of file formats back then, so some (to this day unknown) designer decided to finesse the problem by taking each file and dividing it into three parts. The third part was all of the actual data records of arbitrary size and format. And the first part was an array of relative pointers into entry points of the procedures in the second part . . .

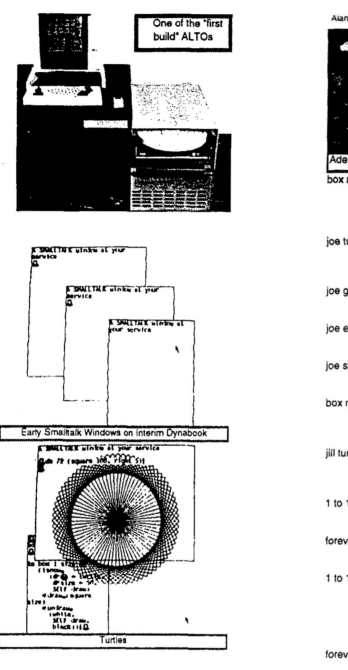

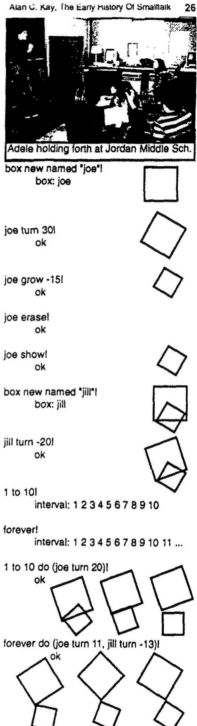

Extract from *The Early History of Smalltalk* by Alan Kay (1993)

What he is explaining here is the essence of the new paradigm of computing where the representation of data and program is held together. Kay is scathing about the clunky way that the <u>agglomerative</u> languages have developed with a strict separation between the coding of the algorithms and the data they need to work on. This is absolutely not the case with LISP, where the program, while running, can construct bits of code and then run them without stopping for breath.

Later in the same text he refers to Bob Barton (the main designer of the B5000 and a professor at Utah), who mentioned:

> The basic principle of recursive design is to make the parts have the same power as the whole. For the first time I thought of the whole as the entire computer and wondered why anyone would want to divide it up into weaker things called data structures and procedures.

Kay's eventual description of his vision of computing was as follows:

> In computer terms, Smalltalk is a recursion on the notion of [the] computer itself. Instead of dividing 'computer stuff' into things each less strong than the whole – like data structures, procedures, and functions which are the usual paraphernalia of programming languages – each Smalltalk object is a recursion on the entire possibilities of the computer. Thus its semantics are a bit like having thousands and thousands of computers all hooked together by a very fast network. Questions of concrete representation can thus be postponed almost indefinitely because we are mainly concerned that the computers behave appropriately, and are interested in particular strategies only if the results are off or come back too slowly.

'Hello world'

In all the programming textbooks published since computer science became a respectable subject, the first chapter begins with one little program – usually only one or two lines long – which prints out the message 'hello world' on the student's output device. In this way the author attempts to start with something really technically simple, but that encapsulates the 'whole idea' of programming and thus can be seen as getting the student to change from a 'user' of

computing to a 'developer', to make the conceptual leap from passive consumer to active designer. This is the Kay concept of *writing being more important than reading* for computer literacy.

Let us consider the way the position of the student changes as they go through this process. To make the process clearer we ignore the fancy details of current programming suites and just think about what happens.

To start with, the student is a user and the machine is 'out there' doing its own thing (running an operating system like Windows or <u>UNIX</u>, providing services like word processors and graphics, talking to printers, networks and so on – all inscrutable activities going on under the hood). Pick up the book ('*Programming in BINGO*'), read the first chapter and you get told to create a text file and save it as 'Myfirst.bng' or whatever it might be. In the old days this might be a primitive text editor, nowadays there is a little Window application with groovy buttons, etc., but no matter. Into this text editor we are told to type:

```
PRINT "Hello World"
```

This is the moment when we have begun to get a little closer to the unknown machine lurking out there. We do not want the program to deliver the exact statement 'PRINT "Hello World"', we want it to respond with 'Hello World'. So we get to understand that the instruction PRINT is us talking to the computer, and then we leave it to the machine to decide how to respond.

There is a little fossiking about to compile and submit the little program to the computer to run it, which we will ignore. Hopefully after this, the message 'Hello World' will appear somewhere in front of us (or maybe it will appear as a 3D hologram hovering over the building opposite – it depends on the computer!).

The joke (an old programmer's ontological conundrum) is thereby to ask the computer to look as though it understands that it is 'in the world', the same world that we are in. It confronts the student with the idea that the dull lump of metal and wires has suddenly woken up as an observer, is gently tapping on its cage as it were, and asking to be let out.

Before we ran the program there were two worlds, our world with a computer in it (World 1), and the

A teletype

computer's own world of computations (World 2). Now there are three, the first two plus another one in which the computer joins us as observers (World 3), using its own world to reflect upon itself as if it is in our world. The one line program has invoked the idea of a self-conscious machine beside us!

The development of graphical user interfaces over the last 30 years has provided a new way of handling this third world. To explore the relationship between World 2 and World 3, it may be useful to dig a little deeper into what goes on in the GUI (graphical user interface).

The development of consensual domains

Structural coupling and the mouse

Let us consider the mouse. In fact we should consider two systems, a computer with a graphical display, and a person with eyes and an arm/hand. As you move your arm/hand to push the mouse around on the table top, a small patch of coloured pixels moves around on the display screen of the computer in front of you. This is such a standard scenario these days that it is difficult to imagine a time when this situation was novel and strange; the development of the 'user interface' from the punched card to the desktop, with all its attendant metaphors, has made the situation seem supremely normal. It is not part of this discussion to contemplate the point and click idea, which derives from work done with bit-mapped displays and light pens at Xerox Pao Alto labs in the 1960s, and Alan Kay's 'Dynabook'. To delve a little deeper into what is going on as you move your arm, we need to be careful about the interaction, which is between two systems.

All the time the GUI is active, the computer is listening out for messages from the various peripherals attached to it. The messages from the mouse (known, of course, as squeaks) are generated by the trackball (or more advanced replacement) in the mouse housing, which rubs against two orthogonally positioned wheels. As these wheels are made to revolve, they each send a stream of squeaks to the computer. These two streams of squeaks are interpreted by the computer program (mouse driver) as:

1. how much the mouse has moved left–right; and
2. how much the mouse has moved forward–back.

This is the *first arbitrary assumption*, that the wheels are at 90 degrees.

This information is purely relative, it only says that the mouse has moved, not where it actually is. The computer has to make another arbitrary assignment sometime, about where the pointer is on the screen. Windows, borrowing from the Mac, borrowing from the Xerox Star, makes the initial pointer location (i.e. where it is when the GUI fires up) to be at the top left hand of the screen, and significantly this is completely unrelated to the actual position of the mouse on the table. This is the *second arbitrary assumption*.

The form of the output device may vary . . .

Meanwhile the GUI software is maintaining the screen display, which means colouring in a block of pixels by assigning colour numbers to a designated area of memory. This block of memory is sufficient to store the colour value for each of the million or so pixels on the screen, but generally there is only one memory location per pixel. To draw the pointer the program has to:

1. work out which pixels will be covered by the pointer icon;
2. stuff these pixels into a temporary holding area; and
3. replace the pixels with those representing the mouse pointer;

as the mouse moves, the program has to:

4. work out the next location for the pointer;
5. restore the original pixels where the pointer just was;
6. copy the memory locations of the next location of the pointer to some small temporary holding area; and
7. redraw the pointer at the next location;

and so on . . .

Meanwhile a sentient human being is on the other end. This human being has a view of the screen and can see the pointer, and can feel and see his/her hand/arm on the mouse. Now the question of how we know where our hand is is bound up with a long learning process since birth, which has trained our nervous system to use tactile signals, muscle tension and feedback to control the arm/hand movement. Evidence that this is a learned response is provided by babies, who hurl their arms about randomly to begin with, until they realise that their arms are part of 'them', and amputees who still feel twinges and so on in missing limbs. However for the purposes of this discussion we will ignore the complex nature of how we learn to control our limbs, and just concentrate on the idea that what is happening is:

1. we look at the screen, observe the pointer and decide where to move it;
2. we exercise our arm/hand, probably out of sight while watching the pointer;
3. as we move our arm we see the pointer move, so we can decide to go on moving our arm, stop, or change direction.

In this case there is a feedback loop between the screen, eye, brain, arm, mouse and pointer. Moving the mouse causes the pointer to move, and the pointer moving tells us how we should move the mouse.

The point of this tedious discussion is that this loop (screen, eye, brain, arm, mouse, pointer) appears to the unenlightened user as a closed, complete loop, with strict logical consequences all down the line. After all, if I move the mouse, does it not move the pointer? However, the loop is not continuous and is, in fact, two loops:

> Mouse squeaks > program > pointer move

> Eye sees > brain > arm move.

Because of the way the mouse is engineered, the two loops appear to be one, but if you turn the mouse around so the tail is towards you instead of away, then the break in the loop is evident – the pointer moves in the opposite way to the mouse because you have invalidated assumption 1 above. Similarly, if you hold the mouse at an angle, and then move it horizontally with respect to the world situation (i.e. the front edge of the desk you are sitting at) the pointer will move diagonally upwards on the screen. Also, if you pick up the mouse and wave it about in the air the pointer fails to move at all (this will not surprise you, though Scotty of StarTrek expected it to work!).

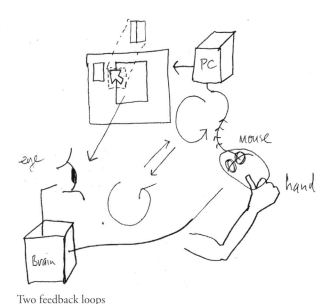

Two feedback loops

Meanwhile the GUI software is maintaining the screen display, which means colouring in a block of pixels by assigning colour numbers·

The pointer over the text

Notice that this magnified screen capture also shows up the 'anti-aliasing' of the text, an algorithm designed to let the human brain/eye see a sharper picture by providing clues that allow the visual cortex to interpolate along curves. Just black and white text looks uncomfortably grainy to the eye. The apparent fuzzyness, therefore, is not a failure to capture the actual pixels, but a faithful rendition of what is presented to the eye. Of course the printed version (which you are reading) does a different thing – it reproduces the text at 1,000 dots per inch rather than 72, as on the screen, so has no need of image enhancement.

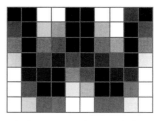

The letter W greatly magnified

Maturana's example of structural coupling

'An example may clarify this situation. Let us consider what happens in instrumental flight. The pilot is isolated from the outside world; all he can do is manipulate the instruments of the plane according to a certain path of change in their readings. When the pilot comes out of the plane, however, his wife and friends embrace him with joy and tell him: "What a wonderful landing you made; we were afraid, because of the heavy fog." But the pilot answers in surprise: "Flight? Landing? What do you mean? I did not fly or land; I only manipulated certain internal relations of the plane in order to obtain a particular sequence of readings in a set of instruments." All that took place in the plane was determined by the structure of the plane and the pilot, and was independent of the nature of the medium that produced the perturbations compensated for by the dynamics of states of the plane: flight and landing are irrelevant for the internal dynamics of the plane. However, from the point of view of the observer, the internal dynamics of the plane results in a flight only if in that respect the structure of the plane matches the structure of the medium; otherwise it does not, even if in the non-matching medium the internal dynamics of states of the plane is indistinguishable from the internal dynamics of states the plane under observed flight. It follows that since the dynamics of states of an organism, or of a nervous system, or of any dynamic system, is always determined by the structure of the system, adequate behaviour is necessarily only the result of a structural matching between organism (dynamic system) and medium.'

(Maturana, 1978: 27–63)

Successful mouse use depends on the two sub-systems (mouse/program/pointer and eye/brain/arm) being coupled together so that a consensus is achieved which results in the apparent feeling that we are actually pushing a little arrow about on the screen with our arm. This is what Humberto Maturana means by 'structural coupling', the two systems are not directly connected, in the sense that we are really pushing the pointer, but they are computing information in two different domains (computer hardware/software and human mind/brain), and in this instance the consensual domain of pointer pushing is constructed.

In this example all the work is being done by the human mind, the computer is just being dumb, and of course is not trying to 'make sense' of what the human is doing, but in the case of two interacting systems, both of which are capable of learning (adjusting their internal operation as it were), then a more open-ended kind of structural coupling can emerge.

It is this emergent consensual domain that is compromised by turning the mouse around, also very heavy processing loads on the computer, which slow down the squeak processing so that it does not keep track of your arm movement, can lead to confusion as the pointer jumps about uselessly since the eye/hand coupling cannot work (this is less of a problem now, but can occur if you try to draw a curve while at the same time rendering 15 radiosity solutions for the Taj Mahal).

But, you will say, 'Isn't it true that the computer is getting information from the user as she moves the mouse around, so its just one loop?' The difficulty here is in the definition of information. Humans think they are influencing the position of the pointer, the computer thinks its getting some squeaks. When you turn the mouse around (or try to work looking at the screen in a mirror – as anyone who has tried to set up a back projection will know), you are not altering the information going to the computer, but the result is non-consensual. So we are not really addressing the computer, we are perturbing it, as the autopoeticists say. Similarly, the computer is perturbing us, by drawing the pointer in different places depending on how we move our arms. This is because, as we move our hand/arm system while holding the mouse, the pointer moves on the screen and our eyes see it – so we assume that we are moving the pointer, just as we would really if we were pushing the pointer around directly.

This is so familiar to us now that we do not notice how weird it is; the new 'haptic' interfaces where you move a wand about in 3D while looking at a 3D world and can feel the obstructions visible on the screen is still a powerful affect, currently available to all via the Nintendo Wii machine's interface – as you make contact with the tennis ball the hand-held puck vibrates convincingly so as to reinforce the illusion and maintain the consensual domain.

Moving the mouse while rotated about the x axis of the real desk top leads to anomalous movement on the virtual desktop

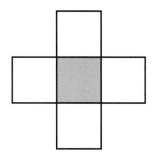 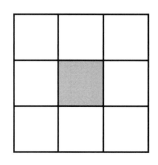

The von Neumann neighbourhood (*left*), the alternative is the eight-neighbour Moore neighbourhood (*right*)

Threshold =

1	2	3	4	5	6	7

```
;; count up the number of coloured patches surrounding a patch
;; "neighbors" is a NetLogo word for the Moore neighbourhood

ask patches [set howmany sum [state] of neighbors]    ;howmany is a count of the neighbors
                                                      ;with state = 1

ask patches ;
[
   ifelse state = 0                                   ;check if the state of this patch
                                                      ;is zero
      [if howmany > 0         [set state 1] ]         ;thing to do if its true set state
                                                      ;1 if neighbors greater than zero
      [if howmany >= threshold [set state 0] ]        ;thing to do if its not true set
                                                      ;state to zero if neighbours greater
                                                      ;than or equal to threshold
]
      ;;if the patch state is 1 then colour it in while otherwise colour it black

ask patches
[
   ifelse state = 1
      [set pcolor white]
      [set pcolor black]
]
```

Who's looking?

Another good example of a kind of computer program which exhibits multiple levels of observer is a Cellular Automaton. This is based on an algorithm which works by taking stock of the immediate surroundings of an object, and then applying some rule based on what it finds (such as 'shall I build a wall or shan't I'?). Such systems tend to be surprising and often display complex global forms, which 'emerge' from the interaction of the many applications of the local rules. While global rules lend themselves well to the methods of procedural algorithms, with the hierarchical linear bias that the good old central processing unit tends to impose, cellular automata often imply a more simultaneous, parallel approach to decision making.

Magic carpet

As an example of the diversity of outcomes that a very simple rule of this type can produce, the 'magic carpet' is an example of a Cellular Automaton which was originally devised by von Neumann and Ulam in the 1940s . It is a model of self-organisation based on a grid of squares which all communicate with their immediate neighbours. Here the field of cells is represented by the PATCHES, a 2D array of square pieces of the graphics window. A cell's neighbours are those patches immediately surrounding the cell. They can be just the four face-joining ones (Moore neighbourhood) or the block of 3 x 3 patches (the von Neumann neighbourhood), see the diagram opposite.

The number of neighbours in this example is set at eight – the von Neumann neighbourhood.

The magic carpet is an example of a Cellular Automaton which is seeded by just one cell in the centre of the cellular array and can develop a range of symmetrical outcomes. The algorithm includes a variable for the threshold number of white cells to trigger the change in Rule 2 (called 'Threshold'). The rules for the magic carpet are as follows – for all cells simultaneously:

- Rule 1 – If a black cell has any white neighbours, it turns white;
- Rule 2 – If a white cell has more than 'Threshold' neighbours, it turns black.

Again, notice that the code addresses just one patch, but NetLogo then applies the rules thus defined to all of the patches simultaneously. (In the NetLogo environment we develop a white pattern on a field of black, in the illustrations these colours have been reversed for clarity.)

- You can set the value of Threshold to any value between 0 and 8.
- The process starts with a field of black cells and one white cell in the middle.
- After several iterations, a symmetrical pattern grows out of the single white cell.

By varying the value of Threshold in the algorithm above, up to seven different patterns can be generated from a single seed cell (0 and 8 are all white/black).

In the magic carpet example what emerges is a symmetrical pattern (if we start from a symmetrical seed) that we can 'see'. We can observe this global outcome of the parallel execution of the little program which lives in all of the patches because our perceptual system picks up on the fact that the grid of squares is ordered so that recurring patterns occur.

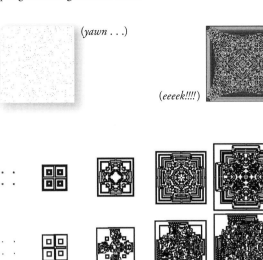

(yawn . . .)

(eeeek!!!!)

Presumably the brain looks for 'meaningful' patterns because they often represent some difference from the natural unordered chaos of the undifferentiated world, and it has turned out over the last four billion years that such structured objects are often food or danger (or both)

Starting from four seeds we get a different symmetrical pattern

Starting from a slightly randomly distributed set of four seeds, this simple patternedness is disturbed and you end up with skewed symmetry

By elaborating the rules a little, such that the value of T (the threshold value) is dependent on the time, new configurations can be generated with second order structure:

26 generations with T = (T mod generation)

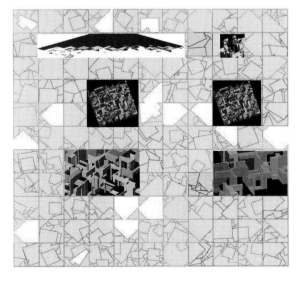

A Cellular Automaton where the 'patches' are solids and the rule is that they are decomposed by chopping bits out of them if their neighbourhood is denser than they are

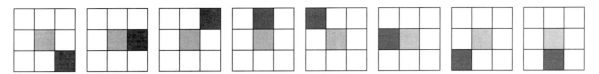

The eight different ways of having a neighbour

Complicatedness versus complexity

The question is, how is it that even though all the little cells have exactly the same rules, the emergent pattern has a global structure? The answer is that, although the patches all have the same program, they have different environments. Right from the start, the creation of the initial seed by turning one cell white means that the eight surrounding patches have slightly different perspectives on the situation, which sometimes means they operate their rules differently. If there were no seed, then there would be no emergent structure. This means that the emergent global structure is dependent on breaking the symmetry of the homogenous field. As this initial asymmetry makes the patches fire their rules differently, then the neighbourhoods of the patches become more different, so leading to differences in the firing of the rules and so on – the mutually amplifying positive feedback scenario we keep on meeting.

The distributed representation allows the algorithm to unfold repeating symmetries that can be observed globally. This observation is external to the model, it is a <u>gestalt</u> that is constructed, in this case by the reader looking at the page opposite. The images have a certain degree of complexity in the sense that a description of the pattern would be quite huge (like Mondrian's experiment to telephone the instructions for painting 'New York boogie woogie' to New York from Europe – it would be a long telephone call much like postcard chess). So, if the output is much larger than the rule, then one is justified in claiming that the total system is 'complex' rather than just complicated. The key thing is the status of the model – it is a distributed model, and it executes in parallel.

A slightly more developed example, taken from the work of a student, shows how this complexity can be transferred into an architectural context. Here the grid of square tiles are seen as an array of spaces. At the beginning of the process each tile assesses its neighbourhood as in the magic carpet above, but instead of just counting up how many tiles are occupied, it calculates the total volume of the eight neighbours. As we are running this in a CAD package, the neighbours are in fact solids that start out as unit cubes. Any cell that has a high volume neighbourhood will chop a chunk out of itself proportional to the density of its neighbours. In this case this is achieved by defining a small cubelet, rotating it and subtracting it from the solids in this cell.

Since your neighbour's neighbourhood includes yourself, then all cells hack chunks of themselves until a predetermined level of density has been reached. In early experiments it was found that cells on the corners and edges of the tiling tended to remain denser than interior cells just because they had fewer neighbours. This effect became more pronounced in 3D versions.

```
if pcolor = white                          ;this patch is currently blank
[
   set d max-one-of neighbors [pcolor]     ;patch with highest patch colour
   set a [pcolor] of d                      ;get the colour of this one
   set b count neighbors with [pcolor = a]  ;how many of this colour?
   set c count neighbors with [pcolor = white] ;how many white ones?
]
ifelse (c + b < 8 )                         ;if the patches of the highest colour
                                            plus white ones don't come to 8
                                            ;then there must be some patches of
                                            another colour so there are >= 2 non
                                            ;white patches in the neighbourhood
                                            ;so this is a boundary


[set boundary true]                         ;its a boundary - mixed colours in the
                                            ;neighbourhood


[set s1 a]                                  ;no its simply surrounded by one colour
                                            ;so colour is set to this colour
```

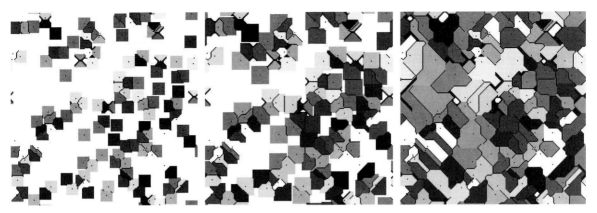

History of a model using a Cellular Automaton to diffuse
colours from seed cells to form tessellations of the plane.
Note that in models of emergent form the end result is only
achieved after the process has run its course – all these models
have a history, unlike the all-in-one top-down global version
as exemplified by the Voronoi algorithm in Chapter 1

Emergent versus globally defined organisations of space

In Chapter 1 there are images of emergent spatial
tilings (drawing bubbles) using small autonomous
parallel computational entities (agents or, in Logo
speak, turtles). In that case the system consisted of an
undifferentiated space with mobile turtles. A similar
effect can be produced using a fixed topology and a
discrete spatial system using the cellular grid of the
Cellular Automaton. The images above were generated
by NetLogo using a Cellular Automaton to diffuse the
Voronoi cells, and using the NetLogo diffuse procedure
to create partial spatial partitions by reaction (diffusion
cells are the emergent boundaries equidistant between
the initial points). In both cases the procedure is to 'leak'
colour or other defining characteristic of a cell out from
a seed spot. When the leaking patches meet a different
shade of grey, then they stop and the place is marked by
a white boundary cell. A series showing this happening
in 3D can be seen on page 48.

The algorithm
All patches are set to white, then some are selected
other colours randomly.

1. All white patches are asked to find out what colour
    the patches in their neighbourhood are.
2. If they are all white, do nothing.
3. If they are a colour, then set yourself to that colour.
4. *But* if you find that there are more than one colour
    in the neighbourhood, then set yourself to white.

So the only trick here is to write a simple code to detect
this boundary condition – see text on page opposite.

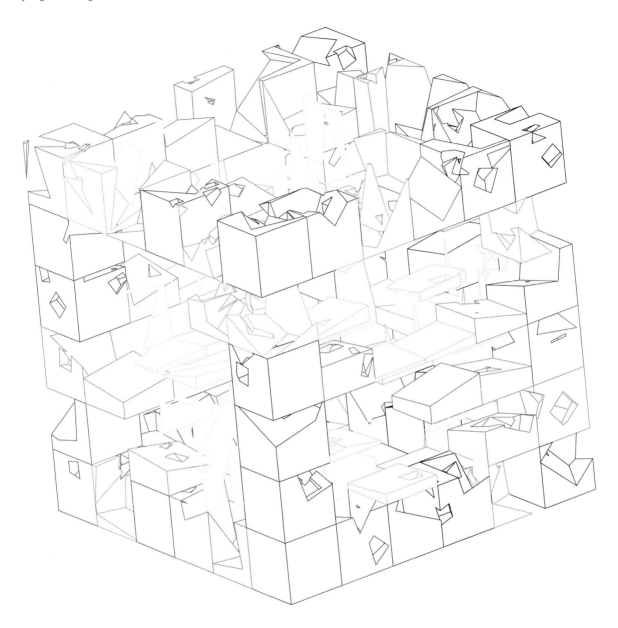

(Gennaro Seannatore, MSc Student, Computing and Design, University of East London, 2008)

The grid-based Cellular Automaton forces all edges to be horizontal, vertical or at 45 degrees. To overcome this artefact the use of the diffusion version results in higher resolution effects. The diffusion algorithm uses a model based on a kind of general leakage of some imaginary 'chemical' from the initiator spots. In these images the colour of the cells of the grid are blended or scaled to reflect the gradual reduction in density of the chemical leading to a rapid fading out of the initial colour. The white boundaries, developed just as in the cellular automata example are more complex.

Three-dimensional Cellular Automata – the magic sponge

The images above Illustrate the three dimensional equivalent of the magic carpet, hence they are magic sponges. Like the magic carpet, it starts with a single seed and the rules in this case are:

1. any empty cell with between 1 and 6 filled-in neighbours comes alive; and
3 any filled cell with between 1 and threshold cells stays alive, otherwise dies.

The threshold in the illustration is 3.

The text of the 3D algorithm is only different in addressing the 26 neighbours of the 3D space that is the cube of cells one cell away around any cell. So where in 2D we have a 3 x 3 block of cells (9 altogether – the von Neumann neighbourhood described above) less the cell itself, giving 8, we now have 3 x 3 x 3 = 27 less one for yourself, otherwise all the rest is the same.

The illustration on the facing page is a 3D development of the subtraction version of the Cellular Automata shown earlier. It displays a wide range of different morphologies achievable with just a simple cutting procedure using a rotated cube. The density rule means that cells on the edges of the system are less cut up than the ones in the middle because they have less neighbours. Compared with the agent-based emergent sphereoids in Chapter 1, these outcomes are considerably more diagrammatic and, for that matter, difficult to control, in the sense that one never knows what one is going to get until the algorithm is run. This is of course the whole point of complex dynamic systems, and what makes them interesting. However, it can be quite frustrating for the student. The trick here, as in all matters when dealing with complex systems, is to get into the habit of *thinking algorithmically*, that is to say to get a feel for how small changes in the generative algorithm will affect the outcome. This is a very different approach from the gradual build up of design moves, or rather it is the same kind of process but with the added advantage of instant feedback on the consequences of the rule changes. In terms of the design process and the educational approach, this is a new way of exploring spatial outcomes - one of the fundamental purposes this book attempts to address.

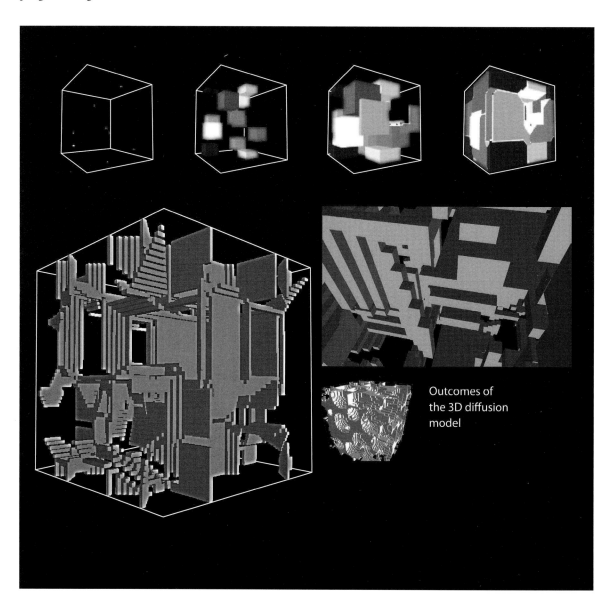

Outcomes of
the 3D diffusion
model

Reaction diffusion in 3D

Using the same algorithm as described earlier, it is also easy to partition 3D space just as in 2D, but instead of using coloured square patches one uses coloured cubes. The history of one run starts with the seed cells from which the expanding cubes arise. When they touch they define boundary plates in 3D instead of the 2D edges. The end product is visualised as a complex sculptural object consisting of the boundary plates.

Once again we are looking at a series of emergent outcomes which are the result of an extremely simple algorithm. The complexity comes from the many different ways that the expanding cubes intersect. This effect is achieved by simply focusing on the process rather than trying to calculate the intersections in some top-down method. This is the same difference as in the emergent tessellation we looked at before, and has the same advantages – we can change the rules and the starting conditions very easily, so that we can concentrate on the implications of different conditions and explore outcomes by exploring rule sets.

As in 2D, the use of diffusion results in higher resolution outcomes.

Raising the level of observation

If one wanted to establish some overall statistics on the outcome (say what is the average volume of the voids in the reaction diffusion examples), then asking the local agents would be useless – they only know what is in their immediate vicinity . In this case one could ask the global observer to count up all patches whose colour is red, then, knowing the overall extents of the world, determine what proportion of available cells are actually red. Other global measures one might like to know about are maybe the total length of the edges in the emergent spheroids, maximum distances between nodes, etc.

So one can conceptualise this cascade of observations as:

Top – person looking at the computer using brain/eye looking at:
　　Global observer/reporter in the program – computer observer of:
　　　　Local agents in the program who just observe their immediate environment.

In the case of the user of the software, this is as far as it goes. If this user is also the programmer, then the whole process is put into a loop where the person can directly change the way the various observations work on the basis of some goal – what the software is for. This is what Papert and Kay were aiming for, the development of the new way of thinking using this new 'mind mirror'.

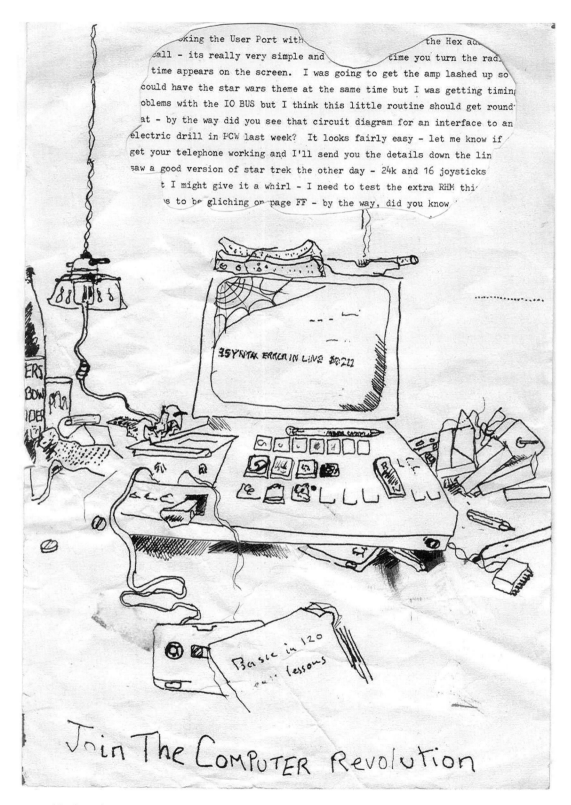

Postcard by the author sometime in 1979–80

Reading and writing, and computer literacy

The main lessons to be learnt from this discussion are that, while the use of the computer in architecture can begin and end with just using the medium, a much more powerful set of experiences can be encouraged if the designer can enter a dialogue with the machine at the level of designing the medium itself, by being able to recast the design intentions and goals in terms that extend the capabilities of the software in front of them. Of course these goals can only be achieved if this interaction is transparent, and self-evident, with a clearly defined way of writing to the machine that is not cumbersome, but also is not toy-like.

In discussions with dissenting colleagues, the main point they make is that current CAD packages contain every possible facility a designer could need, so why should they have to struggle to turn themselves into programmers, wasting valuable learning time in studio. It is true that complex simulations, animations and geometrical transformations are becoming available rapidly, and the abilities of parametric systems to allow formal experiments. There are even plugins for evolutionary algorithms and neural networks. The main reply is along the lines of:

1. There is nothing simple about driving a fully featured simulation/animation package, and to be fully proficient the user will need to spend a great deal of time which will be equally taken out of the design time.

2. Text-based scripting, while presenting an initial hurdle, has an open endedness that overcomes the necessary limitations of any 'canned' interface-driven alternative. With an elegant and powerful language you can make feedback loops between behaviours that allow for a literally infinite set of experiments.

3. The use of Artificial Intelligence and Artificial Life plugins, without any attempt to get involved in understanding their internal structure, is probably not educationally valuable. It is far better to be able to adapt and adjust the core behaviours of such algorithms than to fiddle with the parameters.

Essentially the argument is that of Papert and Kay, why play around on the tip of the iceberg, when with a minimum of effort you can interact with the submerged nine-tenths?

chapter three

The mystery of the machine that invents itself

Having declared that writing simple programs is the best way to describe, represent and understand the shape and patterns of things in the world, we now need to turn to the contemplation of computing machinery. It is traditional to introduce the subject with reference to the Turing machine. This book will follow that tradition by starting with a step-by-step recipe (algorithm) for such a machine. It is based on a JavaScript simulation written by the author and available on the web as a live demo of an adding machine and a pattern recogniser (http://uelceca.net/JAVASCRIPTS/topturing.htm). The mechanics were described by John L. Casti in *Reality Rules: II* (1992), a very clear and well-illustrated explanation that forms the basis of the algorithm.

It must be remembered that the Turing machine was never supposed to exist, it was proposed in the 1930s by Turing as a thought experiment to demonstrate the basic design of a general purpose computing machine. It was necessary to invent the idea of computation as a general thing, and Turing's genius was to define computation at such an abstract level that it could be applied to the widest range of problems. Alonzo Church and Emil Post (two other early twentieth-century mathematicians/philosophers) had, with their theory of functions, also laid the groundwork for this abstract notion of computation that lead indirectly to the definition of LISP – of which more later.

At the beginning of the twentieth century, engineers were busy building special purpose machines for carrying out difficult mathematical calculations, with the original Babbage difference engine as the grandfather of them all. These mathematical machines were programmed by altering the configuration of the machine, as it were redesigning the machine before each run. Systems of gears and pulleys, or wires and relays, were adjusted to the problem in hand, then the machine was run and the results output. In the case of the difference engine, these results (tide tables and other vital compendiums of results) were intended to be printed automatically by a hot metal print works attached to the end of the main 'mill'. A half-finished version is on display at the Science Museum in London. Turing's innovation was to define a machine where the instructions were software not hardware (or ironmongery as it would be called if the English had not relinquished the development of the computer to the Americans). Turing's paper design was eventually built in Manchester, and in America by Von Neumann at Princeton.

The Turing machine is important because it defined the idea of computation in the abstract, and created the idea of the computer as a symbol processing machine and not a calculator. This provided the great generality that allowed the early proponents to dare to think that this might be a model of thinking generally. This lead to the birth of Artificial Intelligence (AI) not long after the development of the first computers. Subsequently, it was determined that whatever goes on in the brain must be to a greater extent the consequence of the firing and communication of synaptic tissue in a great network in the brain (the neural network), but Turing had already had the idea for an artificial neural net (ANN) in unpublished notes from the 1940s (finally published in 1968) – 'intelligent machines', which he was discouraged to pursue by his professor Sir Charles Darwin at the National Physical Laboratory.

The following tale illustrates the way in which a computer invents itself by recapitulating the history of computing. It was written in 1996 about an Apple Macintosh computer, and remains much the same story today.

53

Starting up the Macintosh

In 1936 and 1947 respectively, Alan Turing and John Von Neumann described a universal machine which had the property of being able to read and act on a series of arbitrary symbols, usually represented as a tape (the only machine readable input device people knew about at the time). One of the things it could be proved the machine would be able to do would be to replicate itself, since the actions of the machine (the way it decoded the symbols) could be coded as symbols on the machine readable tape.

One of the axioms of such machines is that it is not possible to prove what such a machine will do by simply inspecting it when it is 'stopped', i.e. not reading the tape. Thus a Mac at rest (without power) contains the components of a Mac, but at that point it could be a great many things.

Not quite, as many of the original designers intended, because even in this quiescent state, a tiny trickle of energy is keeping a few circuits open. The current for these circuits is provided by a small battery, with a life of more than 10 years. These circuits keep the built-in clock going, and monitor the two power switches – one on the keyboard and one at the back. Pressing one of these switches turns the main power on, and the main board is powered with 5V DC. A crystal clock starts to oscillate, and the voltage is regulated to fluctuate in a square wave, which wakes up the microprocessor with its first instructions. The initial instructions, which start the Mac inventing itself are stored in ROM – a form of data storage that is impossible to destroy, and requires no power to stay intact. They consist of an initial 'bootstrap' program which informs the Motorola processor of its existence, and where the memory and main input/output devices are. When the memory

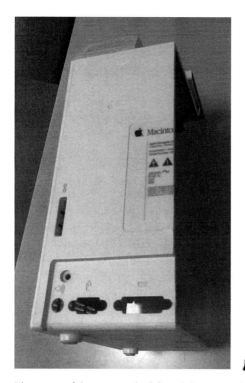 

The casing of the Macintosh (*left*) and the engraved signatures of the design and development team on the inner side (*right*). The Mac established the gold standard for usability and design in 1984 and was famously described by Stephen Levy as 'Insanely great'. The actual machine shown here is the 'Pro version, sliced in two for educational reasons when it was superceded by its decendants.

(RAM) is turned on, it is in a random state, and each cell must be cleared and loaded with data. We have reached the point achieved by the early mainframes in the 1950s. The machine could, at this moment, turn into one of a great many devices, perhaps a dedicated machine tool controller, a brain scanner or an oil refinery valve monitor.

(15 milliseconds have elapsed)
As this is done, the bootstrap program copies the next chunk of instructions from ROM into RAM, and the processor is ordered to begin executing them.

These instructions form the machine operating system or MOS. The main components are:

- the drivers for the data buses (including the hard disk drive);
- the addresses of the <u>quickdraw</u> routines in ROM;
- drivers for the video hardware; and
- an interrupt handler to monitor events among the input devices.

We have now reached the 1970s, a general purpose computer with some graphics capabilities, but no easy way of providing access to them for the user. A command line interface (even more arcane than MS-DOS) lies buried in this code, only reached by programmers who need to activate the programmer's switch (disabled on our machines). To start using the machine we have to wait.

The Mac is now half way to fruition, with all the components necessary in place. They just need organising. About half a second after switching on, the screen clears and is covered with a black and white halftoned one pixel grid. The machine is now capable of using the various devices at its disposal, and has a well-defined repertoire of graphical tools to communicate with the user. It is some kind of graphics based general purpose computer, but exactly how the graphics will be used has yet to be determined.

(About 2 seconds have elapsed)
The organising program lives on the hard disc, and while all this has been going on, the disc has come up to speed, and its own circuitry has been readied to pass data as requested back to the processor. At this point the BIOS requests the hard disk to pass it back mapping information about the contents of the disc, and once

this has been digested, the system file is located and loaded into memory. Once this has been loaded, it begins to run, the screen clears and the Happy Mac face appears.

(10 seconds)
The next software to load is the Window Manager. This software controls all aspects of the graphical user interface (GUI), and underlies all the 'visible' parts of the Mac. Most of this code dates from 1984.

Approximately one megabyte (MB) of software now loads into the RAM, sitting on top of the small amount of MOS and Window Manager code. This software uses the basic elements of Windows, Icons, Menus and <u>Pointers</u> to create the familiar System 7 environment we recognise, and, at last, loads and launches one last component of the Mac , the Finder. The Finder displays the Mac desktop with its icons and windows, and then waits. It is 1996 – 50 years of computer evolution in just under one minute.

The system is now up and running, waiting for the first piece of input to appear from the outside world. A 'personal computer' is essentially an iceberg of software, whose tip is the user interface (the stuff you can see) and at whose depths live the central processing unit operating at a very simple level, beneath the various layers of programs referred to in later sections.

The story set out above describes an actual implementation of a Turing machine, a particular piece of equipment, rather than an abstract idea. The idea that such a machine should be able to replicate itself is demonstrated by the little story in terms of a slow redefinition of a succession of different machines culminating in the Mac, but we need to take a look at the fundamental underlying idea of this machine, so taking a deep breath . . .

The Turing machine

The Turing machine provided the basic plan for a general purpose computer, which however needed to be turned into an actual machine. This was done by John von Neumann, who is credited by the Americans with building the first general purpose computer, ENIAC (Electronic Numerical Integrator And Computer), at Princeton. Von Neumann was a brilliant mathematician (his most famous quote was 'If people do not believe that mathematics is simple, it is only because they do not realize how complicated life is'), who not only designed the overall architecture of the central processing unit that we still use today, but also speculated on such fundamental ideas as a universal replicating computer. To this end he and his friend Ulam devised a series of thought experiments which led to the study of 'Cellular Automata'. It was a characteristic of those early pioneers that they thought big, indeed the foundations of Artificial Intelligence were also set out about the same time, with proposals for thinking machines, artificial brains and so on. It was to be half a century before such projects were even begun, let alone brought to a successful conclusion. (There are still no self-replicating machines that exist in the real world as opposed to the virtual.)

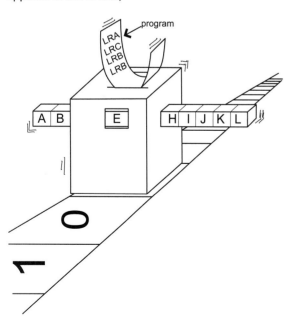

A Turing machine consists of three components:

1.   the tape – an endless strip on which the input symbols are written before the machine begins, and which can be read from and written to as the machine runs;
2.   the read/write head – which can move either backwards or forwards along the tape, either reading off the symbol on the tape, or writing one on to the tape; and
3.   the state table – an array of instructions that determine what the read/write head is going to do (what state it is in).

The entries in the table are named A0, B0, C0, A1, B1, C1. The instructions in the table are of the form <digit, direction, newstate>, where:

*   digit is 0 or 1 (the just read symbol on the tape);
*   direction is R or L or stop(for moving the read/write head right or left);
*   newstate is A B C or stop.

In the example Turing machine, the read/write head can be in one of three *states,* which are labelled A, B and C in the tables that follow. In any state the read head will be over a 0 or a 1, and thus there are six different actions that the machine can perform. Each action is made up of:

*   new symbol to put on the tape;
*   direction to move the tape under the read write head; and
*   new state to be in.

The point to note is that the result of reading a state table entry is to trigger a new action, consisting of state + symbol pair, which then points to a new action and so on.

The read/write head is put into state A and in the addition algorithm the read/write head is positioned over the first 1 found on the tape, reading in the European left to right sense.

The Turing machine for addition

The input tape should contain two groups of ones separated by a zero:

    00011011100000

After the machine has run, the tape will contain a string of ones that will add up to the total:

    00011111000000

The cumulative history of the computation is shown in the window below the state table. The state table which determines what the machine must do depending on what has been read in looks like this (see also the screenshot taken from the previously noted web page).

State	If you read symbol 0	If you read symbol 1
A	Write 1, go Right set state to B	Write 1, go Right set state to A
B	Write 0, go Left set state to C	Write 1, go Right set state to B
C	Stop	Write 0 stop

In the algorithm the code stored in the table is shown in the screen shot

This data are the content of the address or the INSTRUCTION , the addresses of the table are

A0	A1	A	1RB	1RA
B0	B1	B	0LC	1RB
C0	C1	C	stop	0stop

In the code we construct the place to look in the table (the address) by concatenation of the state we are in (A or B or C) with the symbol just read from the tape (0 or 1). So we get 'A' and '0' to give 'A0'. Now 'A0' is a piece of data. But when we evaluate (EVAL) this we can point to the place in the table whose address is A0. The content of the address A0 is 1RB. So every location in the table has both an address and some data, and we can construct a new address using the data. On the next page we work through the way it works step by step.

The input tape should conain two groups of ones separated by a zero.

output 00011111000000

input 00011011100000

type any sequence of 0s and 1s but don't expect it to work unless you follow the rules above

State	symbol 0 read	symbol 1 read
A	1RB	1RA
B	0LC	1RB
C	stop	0stop

Console: this is the record of the progress of the algorythm

```
state A rule null
state A rule R symbol 1
state A rule R symbol 1
state B rule R symbol 0
state B rule R symbol 1
state B rule R symbol 1
state B rule R symbol 1
state C rule L symbol 0
state t rule s symbol 1
```

[Run Machine]   [Reset Tape]

Screenshot of the Turing machine webpage

Start with state set to A and the read/write head positioned over the first 1 on the tape (that is the fourth character in from the left-hand end of the input tape) – the rule at this moment is undefined

state A rule null

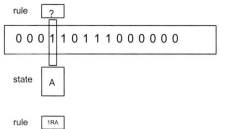

read

The symbol read in from the tape is 1
So construct the new address

= state + symbol = A1

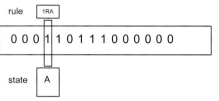

write

The rule at address A1 is 1RA (see the diagram above)

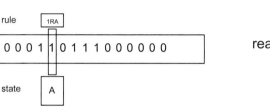

read

This means: 'write a 1 on the tape, move right and go into state A'

symbol 1 rule R state A

now read in the next symbol = it is 1 again
address

= state + symbol = A1

This goes on until we meet a zero on the tape

Read in the next symbol , which is 0

address = **state + symbol = A0**

Rule at address A0 is 1RB

So this means 'write a 1 on the tape and go right and go into state B'

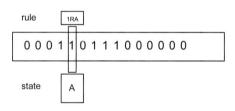

write

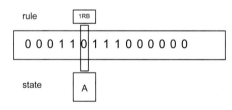

read

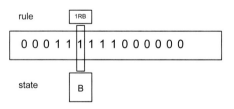

write

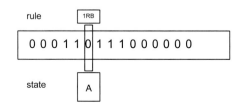

read

We continue to read symbols while staying in state B and writing to the tape with a 1 (we have slipped 4 read cycles here)

We read in the next symbol which is 0 (signalling the end of data)

address = **B0**

Rule at B0 is 0LC
So write a 0 on the tape go left

And change to state C

state C rule L symbol 0

Read in the next symbol – this is a 1 because we have just moved the tape head backwards

address = **C1**

Rule at C1 is S(TOP)
state t rule s symbol 1

So that is it, we terminate

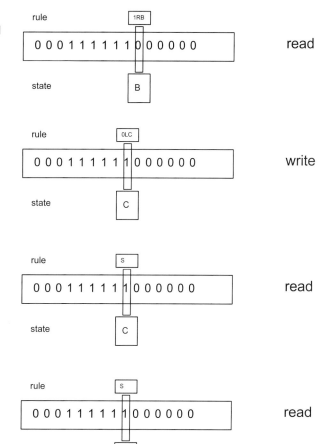

This algorithm works because it relies on the order in which it encounters the ones and zeros on the tape. In state A it overwrites zeros with ones, but then when changed to state B, it gets to stop on reaching a zero.

So the tape which began with two isolated sets of ones now has a single set. This is why it is referred to as the Turing machine for addition – the idea being that if you were to keep a count of the total number of ones on the tape, by the end it would be the result of adding up the two different sets of ones at the beginning.

Phew!

```
while (rule != "s" && state != "t") {

digit = item(counter,thetape)

var rulename = state+digit

   var ruleset = eval("form." + state+digit+ ".value")
   var newdigit = item(0,ruleset)



rule = item(1, ruleset)

state = item(2, ruleset)
   thelength = thetape.length



thetape = thetape.substring(0, counter)+ newdigit + thetape.substring(counter +1,
      thelength)
   form.tape.value = thetape
   form.console.value = form.console.value + "state "+ state +" rule "+ rule + " symbol
      "+ digit +"\n"
   if (rule == "R") {counter = counter +1}
   if (rule == "L") {counter = counter -1}
   if (counter < 0) {
     alert("run out of tape")
     break
     }
}
```

The virtual (perhaps the embodied) Turing machine on the web page is written in JavaScript (it could have been written in a variety of languages, but JavaScript was handy in 1999 for constructing little algorithmic examples on the web – http://uelceca.net/JAVASCRIPTS/topturing.htm). There are a number of things worth noticing here:

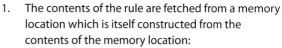

1. The contents of the rule are fetched from a memory location which is itself constructed from the contents of the memory location:
   var ruleset = eval("form." + state+digit + ".value")
   To do this would normally require elaborate programming of a look-up table to get the appropriate rule given the state + tape value, but here, just as in LISP (described in detail later), we can ask the machine to do it for us by passing the symbols to the evaluator built in to Java. This performs the trick of converting the string referred to by state + digit into its name (say A0 or B1) and then asking the datastructure that holds the state table to return the contents of the address thus constructed.

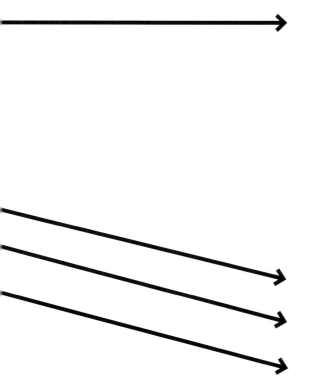

2. The position of the tape head is under the control of the rule, which is pointed to by the procedure in 1.
3. The particular rule is chosen depending on the position of the tape head.
4. Changing the contents of the tape will alter the order in which the rules are invoked (alter the procedure for calculating addresses).
5. Changing the number and contents of the rules will alter the contents of the tape.

What this means is that the overall architecture of the machine (as computer engineers say) does not have to change at all to accommodate a new problem. The values in the addresses are altered, the number of addresses can be stretched, the tape can be any length, but the basic architecture of program counter, addressing scheme and memory remain the same.

This was the breakthrough that led to the development of the von Neumann machine (the stored program computer), a copy of which sits on your desk right now. The essential cleverness about the Turing machine, the 'fundamental flip', is that, as we have seen, *an ADDRESS of a new INSTRUCTION can be assembled out of the contents of the current instruction.* Thus everything points to everything else, and, since the contents of the address can be altered, there is no limit to the complexity of algorithm that can be programmed.

Douglas Hofstadter (in *Metamagical Themas*, 1996) cites an example of a salt packet which provides infinite regress (like standing between two mirrors). The shaker lady is holding a packet of salt, which shows a picture of a shaker lady holding a packet of salt, which shows . . .

The old man said 'I'll tell you a story, once upon a time an old man came up to a young girl and said "I'll tell you a story, once upon a time an old man . . ."'

Recursion

As a further development of the notion that the text of the algorithm is a useful form of architectural representation, we now consider the mechanism of recursion. Recursion has to be distinguished from the simple LOOP or sausage machine which simply repeats the same set of instructions over and over. You can do a loop with recursion, but you can also do more interesting things, thus recursion is the general idea with loops as a subset. Once you have grasped recursion, loops are banal. Examples of recursive algorithms can be found in the biological sciences, where 'self-similarity' has been exploited to model many growing things, from trees and cities to chrysanthemums. Douglas Hofstadter's (1979) canonical introduction to Artificial Intelligence, *Godel Escher Bach*, uses the painter M. E. Escher's infinite staircases and tilings as an example of recursion and self-referential diagrams.

A *recursive function* is a set of instructions that contain a reference to themselves. To do recursion, you have to use a language that uses symbols to stand for 'chunks' of program, so recursion is a higher level construct than simple looping. Recursive algorithms allow one to model self-similar objects, where the rules for making a little bit are the same (but perhaps at a different scale) from the rules for making the whole.

There is one barrier to understanding recursion which has to do with the way the code is written. In simple loops and, for instance, the little bits of code presented so far, they pretty much match the way one can imagine the computer working. We write down:

```
start

   do something
   do something
   do something

stop
```

In Chapter 1, the NetLogo ASK is a little bit different because, although it seems to be addressing one turle or patch, it is in fact addressing them all, but in an unseen loop. However, this is not so hard to comprehend. We can easily imagine it means:

```
start
for each turtle

   do something
   do something
   do something

stop
```

In a recursive routine the representation on the page does not match what happens when the function runs, for instance:

```
to grow

   if needed
   grow

end
```

So the text on the page just refers to one grow function, but somehow it is going to call itself, so there are really two copies of grow and that one will also call itself. The possible result of four recursions is set out on the next page.

This also introduces the notion that, unless we put in a *condition*, this self-referential recursion will go on for ever – the endless loop dreaded by all programmers that can only be broken by chucking the computer out of the window.

Not only that, a recursive routine uses its own output as input for the following recursion's input, so essentially the function:

1. accepts an input;
2. does some processing on that input;
3. which is then passed on to the same function for further processing;

and so on . . .

Unfolding the history of a recursive algorithm

```
to grow

        if needed grow                          1st recursion

            to grow

                if needed grow                  2nd recursion

                    to grow

                    if needed grow              3rd recursion

                        to grow

                        if needed grow          4th recursion

                        grow                    At this point it must be assumed
                                                that needed is no longer true
                        endgrow                 and the algorithm

                    endgrow                     unwinds

                endgrow                         down and back

            endgrow                             to the original call

end
```

Recursion is like encapsulation – the embedding of one thing into a copy of itself. But I also sometimes find it helpful to explain the principle in terms of NESTING. This is best explained with reference to shopping bags. When you empty the bags of shopping after coming home, you end up with a lot of bags.

What you can do after this is to put all the bags into one of the bags, so that you have a bag of bags. If you do this every Saturday morning for several weeks, you may have many bags of bags, so you could put all the bags of bags into a bag, ending up with a bag of bags of bags. This is a recursive situation and can be diagrammed as:

Simple start position – some bags:

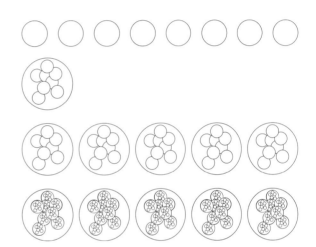

> bag bag bag bag bag bag bag bag bag bag

First recursion put all bags into a bag

> BAG(bag bag bag bag bag bag)

where the enclosure is represented by brackets.

Second recursion – a lot of bags of bags:

> BAG(bag bag bag...) BAG(bag bag bag
>   bag...) BAG(bag bag bag bag...)...

Third recursion –put the bags of bags into a bag:

> BAG(BAG(bag bag bag bag bag) BAG(bag bag
>   bag bag)...)...

In the bag system, the rule is about encapsulation (or bagging up) so that as you go on, the individual bags get ever deeper in the structure of hierarchically embagged bags.

A LISP interlude

In the notes following, the examples are given using AutoCAD's version of LISP – AutoLISP. This is a standard version with some extras for communication with AutoCAD. Examples of its use can be found in the following pages.

The fundamental (the only) thing that LISP does is to build symbol strings called *lists*, which are written as:

```
(..............)
```

The LISP engine can do two things with a list, it can either *evaluate* it or *quote* it. LISP's natural inclination is to evaluate a list, so that presented with a list such as:

```
(+ 1 2 )
```

it will assume that:

1. the first symbol is the name of a function in its library of common things it knows how to do; and
2. that the remainder of the symbols are arguments to that function.

The + function adds together the remaining arguments until the list is ended or another list is encountered (of which more later). The result of (+ 1 2) is unsurprisingly 3, echoed back on the commandline. This is the result of the evaluation of (+ 1 2).

LISP, being a very ancient language, uses a very simple stack-based evaluation scheme. As LISP reads the text, it pushes arguments onto a first-in last-out stack, like a spring-loaded plate holder. When the list ends, the stack is emptied and the result pops out. This allows for the saving of intermediate results during recursion (of which more later).

If we type:

```
(+ 1 2 (+ 1 2))
```

we get 6 because (+ 1 2) evaluates to 3, so the expression is really (+ 1 2 3). Notice the *nested brackets*.

Cartoon from xkcd.com by Randall Munroe

Variables
The most used function in LISP is a cheat:

```
(SETQ var expression), e.g. (setq a 3)
```

It means set quote or 'don't evaluate', and brings in the idea of a variable because a variable is a name for something and not the thing itself. If you type (+ x y) on the command line you will get:

```
Command: (+ x y)
; error: bad argument type: numberp: nil
```

as an evaluation because x and y are not part of LISP's vocabulary, they do not evaluate to anything. To make symbols like x and y evaluate to something, we have to bind them to actual evaluatable lists or symbols (usually referred to in LISP as *atoms*), without automatically invoking LISP's predilection for trying to evaluate everything.

Why it is a cheat is that you could actually use SET, the more general assignment operator, and say (SET 'x 3), meaning set the quoted value of symbol x to evaluate to 3. The ' mark is the quote, meaning 'don't believe me, I'm telling you he said it !' or *don't evaluate* to the LISP engine. Typing '(x)' on the command line will just produce:

```
Command: (x)
; error: no function definition: x
```

Below is what AutoCAD does when we type in the two phrases (the exclamation mark is AutoCAD's method for asking the value of x):

```
Command: (set 'x 3)
3
Command: (setq x 3)
3
Command: !x
3
```

Being ancient and simple, it will come as no surprise to learn that LISP does not really have any variables, just loads of lists, made of other lists, and at the bottom the few atoms of the language – numbers, simple functions and, of course, the list processing functions.

AutoCAD justified their adoption of LISP as a macro programming language for AutoCAD on the basis that points in 3D space are triplets and can be naturally represented as a list (x y z). Actually it was probably because it was very economical in memory use and easily picked up in any university in the late 1970s. Nowadays they push C++ for programmers and BASIC for the rest of us. LISP continues to be useful because of the way that genetic programming function trees can be represented in LISP. As LISP is so keen to evaluate everything, it will even evaluate the data it makes itself, which is to say that for LISP there is no difference between data and programs (but then you never thought there was anyway did you?).

The point in space can be expressed as a list (0 0 0) or more properly '(0 0 0), so that you do not get an awkward cough from the LISP engine as it tries to evaluate the non-existent function '0', and to reference the things inside this list we have some functions to help:

```
(setq p (list 10 25 34))
(car p)  10
(cdr p)  (25 34)
(cadr p) the car of the cdr of p
    (car(cdr p))  25
(caddr p) the car of the cdr of the cdr of p
    (car(cdr(cdr p)))  34
```

All these functions are built out of the basic two:

```
(car list) – this first thing in a list
and (cdr list) – all the rest
```

Note, 'things' can be lists or atoms.

Luckily these clumsy operators have been extended by NTH and FOREACH. (nth 3 p) gives the fourth element of list p and you can run through a whole list:

```
(foreach  coord p (print coord))
```

Building a turtle language: an introduction to one of the most venerable languages in computing

To illustrate the idea of constructing a simple vocabulary for the computer to understand, the following notes use a version of LISP that can be used to drive the drawing functions in AutoCAD. First the main words of the vocabulary will be constructed, using the function definition facilities of LISP. Defining functions in LISP is a way of extending the language so that the programmer can do something new. In this case, the new thing is to be able to draw lines and rotate the coordinate system. The following notes culminate in an illustration of the use of EVAL and recursion to generate complex shapes based on a simple recursive rewrite function. Using the 'command' LISP function, we can call up all the things AutoCAD knows how to do, for instance:

```
(command "_line" '(0 0 0) '(1 0 0) "")
```

is the equivalent to typing `line` on the command line and supplying the origin as 0,0,0 and the end as 1,0,0 . This will draw a line 1 unit long (i.e. along the x axis of the current coordinate system), starting at the coordinate systems' origin. This can be used as the body of a new function called 'f':

```
(defun f (  )
   (command "_line" '(0 0 0) '(1 0 0) "")
)
```

this can be called from the command-line by typing `(f)`.

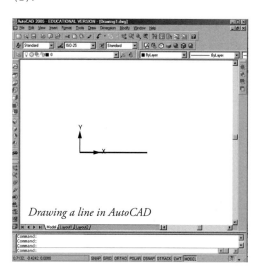

Drawing a line in AutoCAD

We could draw more than one line by calling the function f many times, but they would all be drawn on top of each other. There are many ways of getting round this, but we are going to adopt the convention that *after* drawing anything we move the coordinate system origin to the end of what we have drawn. This is the *turtle drawing mode* we need for later exercises. Moving the coordinate system can be done with the UCS origin command:

```
(command "_ucs" "o" '(1 0 0))
```

so the function now looks like this:

```
(defun f ( )
(command "_line" '(0 0 0) '(1 0 0)"")
(command "_ucs" "o" '(1 0 0))
)
```

Making the line turn

To do something a bit more interesting, we can also write a function to rotate the coordinate system so that the line will be drawn in other directions than horizontal. Turning is implemented by rotating the coordinate system because this captures the local nature of the turn, which is from the turtle's perspective. After a turn the turtle is still going 'forwards' after all.

```
(command "_ucs" "z" 90)
```

is how we can rotate the plan (z) axis of the drawing by 90 degrees positive (equivalent to turning left from the perspective of the line). To turn right, use –90. So that gives us two new functions.

This function turns the coordinate system left:
```
(defun l ()
   (command "_ucs" "z" 90)
)
```
and this one turns it right:

```
(defun r ()
   (command "_ucs" "z" -90)
)
```

so to draw a staircase we can write

```
(f)(l)(f)(r)(f)(l)(f)(r)(f)  ...
```

There is one last thing we can do to make the functions more general, replace the *constants* 90 and –90 by a *variable* that can be altered:

```
(setq ang 90)
```

This will create a global variable `ang` which we can change to effect all the functions that use it:

```
(defun r ()
  (command "_ucs" "z" (- ang))
)

(defun l ()
  (command "_ucs" "z"  ang)
)
```

These three functions are the base for our turtle drawing interpreter. They provide a symbology for the computer to be able to make up expressions in the language.

The systems which will be explored here are cast in the form 'from your current position and heading do the following'. This can be reapplied after the move, as the instructions do not specify where to start from (assumed to be 'here'), only what to do next.

So the symbol string F L F L F L F (forward left forward left forward left forward) should draw a square of unit side, if the angle is 90 degrees. To do this we can type:

```
(f)(l)(f)(l)(f)(l)(f)
Command:  (f)(l)(f)(l)(f)(l)(f)
```

Notice in the illustration how the UCS icon is turned upside down as a consequence of rotating it at each corner. The text is taken from the text window and shows how AutoCAD has rotated the coordinate system for the lines to be drawn in the right orientation.

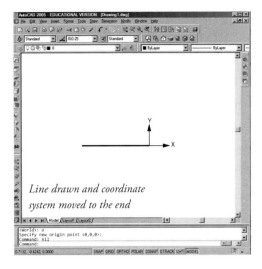

Line drawn and coordinate system moved to the end

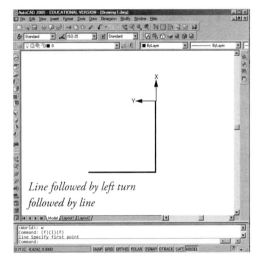

Line followed by left turn followed by line

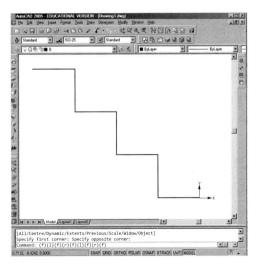

Try adding the word delicious in front of the axiom tomatoes and see what a difference it makes to the first course. Experiment with different production rules.....

Console - this is the record of the progress of the algorithm

```
New Rule
 tomatoes
New Rule
  with linguine and basil
New Rule
   with linguine runny with delicious pesto  basil
New Rule
    with linguine yummy and delicious with made of runny and
yummy pasta pesto  basil
```

Number of levels of recursion `5`

Axiom - the initial seed `tomatoes`

production rules replace

this with   this

`tomatoes`	`tomatoes with linguine and basil`	Run Machine
`and`	`runny and with delicious pesto`	
`delicious`	`y and ymmy pasta and tomatoes`	
`runny`	`and delicious tomatoes and pasta`	

`Reset fields`

(*above*) Screenshot of the Itallian Dinner Javascript webpage
(*right*) Sample output from five recursions of the system

Output data
tomatoes
Output data
tomatoes with linguine and basil
Output data
tomatoes with linguine and basil with linguine
runny and with delicious pesto basil
Output data
tomatoes with linguine and basil with linguine
runny and with delicious pesto basil with
linguine yummy and delicious tomatoes and pasta
runny and with delicious pesto with made of runny
and yummy pasta and tomatoes pesto basil
Output data
tomatoes with linguine and basil with linguine
runny and with delicious pesto basil with
linguine yummy and delicious tomatoes and pasta
runny and with delicious pesto with made of
runny and yummy pasta and tomatoes pesto basil
with linguine yummy runny and with delicious
pesto made of runny and yummy pasta and tomatoes
tomatoes with linguine and basil runny and
with delicious pesto pasta yummy and delicious
tomatoes and pasta runny and with delicious pesto
with made of runny and yummy pasta and tomatoes
pesto with made of yummy and delicious tomatoes
and pasta runny and with delicious pesto yummy
pasta runny and with delicious pesto tomatoes
with linguine and basil pesto basil
Output data
tomatoes with linguine and basil with linguine
runny and with delicious pesto basil with
linguine yummy and delicious tomatoes and pasta
runny and with delicious pesto with made of
runny and yummy pasta and tomatoes pesto basil
with linguine yummy runny and with delicious
pesto made of runny and yummy pasta and tomatoes
tomatoes with linguine and basil runny and
with delicious pesto pasta yummy and delicious
tomatoes and pasta runny and with delicious pesto
with made of runny and yummy pasta and tomatoes
pesto with made of yummy and delicious tomatoes
and pasta runny and with delicious pesto yummy
pasta runny and with delicious pesto tomatoes
with linguine and basil pesto basil with linguine
yummy yummy and delicious tomatoes and pasta
runny and with delicious pesto with made of
runny and yummy pasta and tomatoes pesto made
of yummy and delicious tomatoes and pasta runny
and with delicious pesto yummy pasta runny and
with delicious pesto tomatoes with linguine and
basil tomatoes with linguine and basil with
linguine runny and with delicious pesto basil
yummy and delicious tomatoes and pasta runny
and with delicious pesto with made of runny
and yummy pasta and tomatoes pesto pasta yummy
runny and with delicious pesto made of runny and
yummy pasta and tomatoes tomatoes with linguine
and basil runny and with delicious pesto pasta
yummy and delicious tomatoes and pasta runny
and with delicious pesto with made of runny and
yummy pasta and tomatoes pesto with made of
yummy and delicious tomatoes and pasta runny and
with delicious pesto yummy pasta runny and with
delicious pesto tomatoes with linguine and basil
pesto with made of yummy runny and with delicious
pesto made of runny and yummy pasta and tomatoes
tomatoes with linguine and basil runny and
with delicious pesto pasta yummy and delicious
tomatoes and pasta runny and with delicious pesto
with made of runny and yummy pasta and tomatoes
pesto yummy pasta yummy and delicious tomatoes
and pasta runny and with delicious pesto with
made of runny and yummy pasta and tomatoes pesto
tomatoes with linguine and basil with linguine
runny and with delicious pesto basil pesto basil

Building the interpreter's rewrite engine

The Italian dinner

In <u>Douglas Hofstadter</u>'s *Metamagical Themas* (a compendium of essays he wrote for *Scientific American* when he took over from Martin Gardner), there is a typically funny, but useful, introduction to <u>production</u> systems based on a recursive replacement algorithm to generate Italian recipes.

Production systems are examples of recursive algorithms, that is, they are functions that use as input the output of their own results on earlier operations. The most general way of characterising a production system is to see it as a formal language based on symbol manipulation. They have much in common with formal systems in logic, in that:

1. they start with an axiom, which is a given of the formal system;
2. there are a set of statements in the formal system which can be thought of as theorems of the system; and
3. there are a set of rules for transforming any statement which is part of the formal system into any other, using replacement rules.

In the Italian dinner, the axiom is of course *tomatoes*. You can see from the screen shot of the page (on the same website as the other examples – http://uelceca.net/JAVASCRIPTS/topturing.htm), that there are four replacement rules:

Left-hand side		Right-hand side
tomatoes	*is replaced by*	tomatoes with linguine and basil
and	*is replaced by*	runny with delicious pesto
delicious	*is replaced by*	made of runny and yummy pasta and tomatoes
runny	*is replaced by*	yummy and delicious tomatoes and pasta

Note that in order for this to work, we have to have at least one word in the right-hand side that matches one of the words in the left-hand side. If we do not do this, then the production system will not catch, and it will fail to expand into the florid ingredients list in the panel to the left. To change this production system into an automatic Chinese menu generator, we can change the axiom to rice, and the left-hand sides to fried, egg, noodle, pork, and so on, with the right-hand sides perhaps as soy sauce, chicken, etc.

Also, note that the production grows exponentially as the recursions build up because the replacement strings (right-hand sides) are generally longer than the left-hand sides. The sequence is a kind of frillyfication of the axiom.

It is also possible to notice a degree of repetition that has a pattern which is difficult to pin down. It is not just a repeated list of ingredients, but phrases tend to crop up in slightly different contexts – sometimes delicious tomatoes, then pasta and tomatoes pesto, and pasta and tomatoes:

```
basil with linguine yummy and delicious
tomatoes and pasta runny and with
delicious pesto with made of runny and
yummy pasta and tomatoes pesto basil with
linguine yummy runny and with delicious
pesto made of runny and yummy pasta and
tomatoes
```

What is happening here is that the process of embedding extends the axiom in complex ways as the expanding string of ingredients is reprocessed at each recursion.

The following discussion will take as its starting point the idea that the following symbols will draw three sides of a square: (F L F L F). A production system begins with an axiom, something that can be used as a seed to start the process of expansion. In this case the axiom is F – draw a line:

```
(setq axiom '(F))
```

The replacement rule is: each time you see an F in the current string, replace it with F L F L F.

Therefore, presenting the replacement rule with F will generate the symbol string F L F L F (not just a bag but a bag of bags).

So that is just the basic drawing. If we then operate the replacement rule again, so that every F turns into F L F L F L (not just a bag of Fs but a bag of bags of Fs), we get

1 recursion (F L F L F L)

Re-presenting this string to the replacement engine we get

2 recursions (F L F L F L L F L F L F L L F L F L F L L)

and a third time

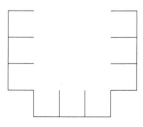

3 recursions (F L F L F L L F L F L F L L F L F L F L L L F L F L F L L F L F L F L L F L F L F L L L F L F L F L L F L F L F L L F L F L F L L L)

Rewriting the line drawing system

The next section tries to explain this process by means of illustrating the building of a string rewriting system, also known as a production system, to construct some text recursively which is then evaluated to draw self-similar objects of some complexity.

The example chosen is a kind of Lindenmayer System, or L-system, first elaborated by the Hungarian botanist Aristid Lindenmayer, whose most accessible book is *The Algorithmic Beauty of Plants* (1968). Here only the simplest type is discussed. During the 1980s they were used extensively to model complex emergent structures of branching systems (to be discussed in the next chapter in the context of evolutionary algorithms because of the way one can evolve these strings using genetic programming – a way of evolving computer programs, the ultimate example of code rewriting itself).

In this example we will write some code that writes some code, and then uses LISP's EVAL function to execute the new code to produce a drawing. The rest of this section will look at a particular production system that expands sentences of drawing symbols rather than Italian recipe ingredients, our simple vocabulary of F, L and R

Having a simple vocabulary is all very well, but to do anything interesting we need to get the computer to do a bit more work for us, so as to be able to experiment with more complex things than circles and squares.

L-systems are formal expressions in symbolic notation which consist of a set of production rules, such that a given input is bound to result in a particular output. Production rules, in general, can be lengthening or shortening (the latter could be called reduction rules) or both. L-systems have lengthening rules, each operation of the rules results in a longer string.

In L-systems, the rules are replacement rules, with two parts – the left-hand side and the right-hand side, which can be written as:

> LHS>>RHS

The symbols in the rules are turtle line drawing movements of which there are three that have been developed above: R, L and F.

The left-hand side is the 'thing to recognise' and the right-hand side is the thing to replace it with. The general form of a production rule is:

> output_list = input_list(LHS >> RHS)

or

> replace all occurrences of LHS in input_list with RHS.

So in bag terminology, the LHS is like a single bag, and the replacement of its occurrences is like making a collection of bags in a bag. If the right-hand side does not contain any examples of the left-hand side, then the string goes unchanged. If it does, then the next string will contain more versions of the left-hand side and will trigger a cascade of lengthening strings, which means in L-systems an increasing amount of geometry.

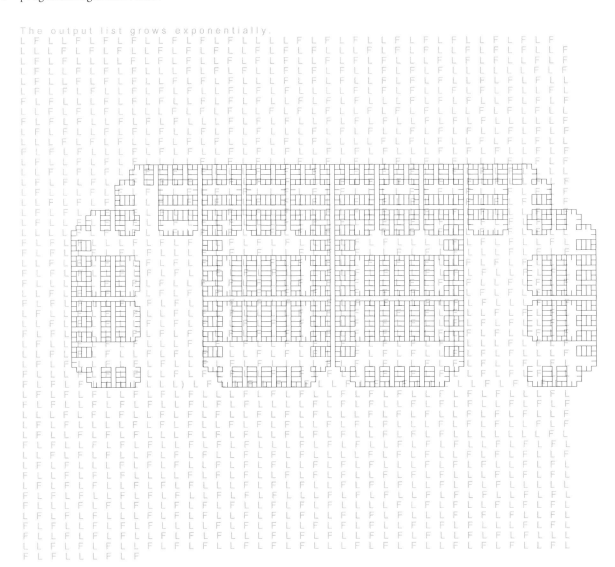

Seven recursions

After seven recursions

The image on the facing page, in common with all such replacement systems, is interesting for the way the initial motif, the three-sided square, is subtly transformed into a much more complex object, but still has the three sides we began with.

There are a number of emergent patterns that can be observed to have an architectural property, such as the reflected repeated bays of cells, and the articulation of the corners which suggests a way of treating the change of direction both internally and externally. If these observables strike any chords, then it points to architecture itself being partly of a self-similar nature. Large plans often contain both repeats and nested structures of cells, with often some correspondence across scales. To get from this simple diagram to something nearer to a useful plan would, of course, require a few more rules, but the point to note here is that even very simple shapes can generate an emergent outcome that captures some of the complexity of architectural objects.

Building the rewrite rule

So, how does this work? As in the Italian dinner, we have two symbol strings or lists called LeftHandSide and RightHandSide, which represent:

- LHS = the thing in the input list to be recognised (here F); and
- RHS= the thing with which we will replace all occurrences of LHS in the input list (here F L F L F).

And two different lists:

- the input list (which is initially the AXIOM (in this case F); and
- the output list (which is the input list with all the Fs turned into F L F L F L).

We have to define a function which does this, and also feed the output list back into the function as the input list.

Suppose we have the current input list called 'inprod' and the RHS and LHS named as before, what we want to do to make a new list we shall call 'newp' by saying:

- make an empty list – call it newp;
- take each symbol – call it s in the inprod one at a time;
- with each s, check to see of it equals the LHS;
- if it does, then add RHS to the newp;
- otherwise just add s to newp.

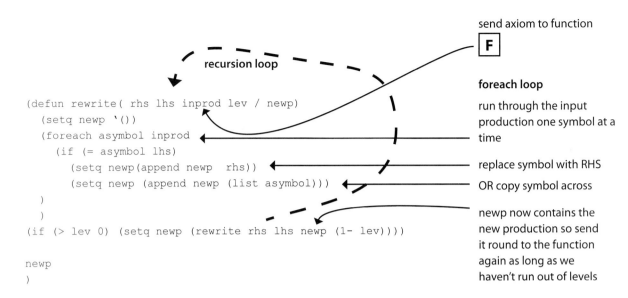

send axiom to function

F

```
(defun rewrite( rhs lhs inprod lev / newp)
   (setq newp '())
   (foreach asymbol inprod
      (if (= asymbol lhs)
         (setq newp(append newp  rhs))
         (setq newp (append newp (list asymbol)))
      )
   )
(if (> lev 0) (setq newp (rewrite rhs lhs newp (1- lev))))
```

recursion loop

foreach loop

run through the input production one symbol at a time

replace symbol with RHS

OR copy symbol across

newp now contains the new production so send it round to the function again as long as we haven't run out of levels

```
newp
)
```

TRACE of what happens with three recursions

Select objects:
Command: no of recursions3
Entering (REWRITE (F L F L F L) F (F) 3)
  Entering (REWRITE (F L F L F L) F (F L F L F L) 2)
   Entering (REWRITE (F L F L F L) F (F L F L F L L F L F L F L L F L F L F L L) 1)
    Entering (REWRITE (F L F L F L) F (F L F L F L L F L F L F L L F L F L F L L L F L F L F L L F L F L
    F L L F L F L F L L F L F L F L L L) 0)

Result:
   (F L F L F L L F L F L F L L F L F L F L L L F L F L F L L F L F L F L L F L F L F L L L F L F L F L L F L F L F L L F L F L F L L L L
    F L F L F L L F L F L F L L F L F L F L L L F L F L F L L F L F L F L L F L F L F L L L F L F L F L L F L F L F L L F L F L F L L L L
    F L F L F L L F L F L F L L F L F L F L L L F L F L F L L F L F L F L L F L F L F L L L F L F L F L L F L F L F L L F L F L F L L L L)
Result:
   (F L F L F L L F L F L F L L F L F L F L L L F L F L F L L F L F L F L L F L F L F L L L F L F L F L L F L F L F L L F L F L F L L L L
    F L F L F L L F L F L F L L F L F L F L L L F L F L F L L F L F L F L L F L F L F L L L F L F L F L L F L F L F L L F L F L F L L L L
    F L F L F L L F L F L F L L F L F L F L L L F L F L F L L F L F L F L L F L F L F L L L F L F L F L L F L F L F L L F L F L F L L L L)
Result:
   (F L F L F L L F L F L F L L F L F L F L L L F L F L F L L F L F L F L L F L F L F L L L F L F L F L L F L F L F L L F L F L F L L L L
    F L F L F L L F L F L F L L F L F L F L L L F L F L F L L F L F L F L L F L F L F L L L F L F L F L L F L F L F L L F L F L F L L L L
    F L F L F L L F L F L F L L F L F L F L L L F L F L F L L F L F L F L L F L F L F L L L F L F L F L L F L F L F L L F L F L F L L L L)
Result:
   (F L F L F L L F L F L F L L F L F L F L L L F L F L F L L F L F L F L L F L F L F L L L F L F L F L L F L F L F L L F L F L F L L L L
    F L F L F L L F L F L F L L F L F L F L L L F L F L F L L F L F L F L L F L F L F L L L F L F L F L L F L F L F L L F L F L F L L L L
    F L F L F L L F L F L F L L F L F L F L L L F L F L F L L F L F L F L L F L F L F L L L F L F L F L L F L F L F L L F L F L F L L L L)
```
```

To do this in AutoLISP we can use the *foreach* function to run through the incoming production. The LISP below should be read as 'for each symbol s in list inprod':

```
(foreach asymbol inprod
```

Then, with the individual symbol from the production called s, we compare it to the left-hand side – 'if s equals lhs', expressed in Miltonic Lispian prose 'Equals asymbol the lhs?':

```
  (if (= Asymbol  lhs)
    (setq newp(append newp rhs))
    (setq newp (append newp (list
        Asymbol)))
  )
```

The two alternatives to the question are set out, first the one to do if it is true, second the one to do if it is not.

That covers doing it once. To do it more, we write the loop inside a function and let it call itself. This, being interpreted, means:

1. Run through input inprod picking one symbol at a time:
    - if a symbol matches the left hand side;
    - then append the "right hand side" symbols to the new production;
    - otherwise append the symbol to the new production.
2. If we still have more recursions to go:
    - make the new production equal to the *recursive call to this function*;
    - otherwise drop out of the function *passing back the value of the production*.
3. Exit function with new production.

The italic emphasis is in need of explication. The main thing to remember is that a recursive function calls itself. What happens when a computer program calls itself? The problem is that a computer program occupies a particular place in memory, and its associated variables are also placed in a particular location (determined by the compiler). If you just overwrite the memory locations with the new call, we will loose the intermediate calculations that successive calls generate (i.e. we will only collect the last recursion). Thus, the *stack* was invented, which holds all the intermediate calculations for all the recursive calls (the old spring-loaded plate analogy). Thus, every recursive call invokes a new copy of the parameters and their results, which stacks up until the recursive call is stopped, at which point the whole stack unwinds, accumulating the complete result.

```
(defun F ()
(command "line" '(0 0 0) '(1 0 0) "")
(command "ucs" "o" '(1 0 0))
)

(defun L()
(command "ucs" "Z" (- ang))
)
(defun R()
(command "ucs" "Z" ang)
)
```

Functions F L and R are the basic drawing functions for Forward Left and Right – basic turtle drawing functions

```
(defun rewrite( rhs lhs inprod lev / newp)
(setq newp '())
(foreach s inprod
       (if (= s lhs) (setq newp(append newp  rhs))
(setq newp (append newp (list s)))
)
 )
(if (> lev 0) (setq newp (rewrite rhs lhs newp (1- lev))))
 newp
)
```

The rewrite function is the main engine of the whole process, recursively expanding the original axiom

```
(defun drawit  (thelist)
       (if (> thelist nil)
            (progn
                (eval    (list(car thelist)))
                (drawit(cdr thelist))
            )
       )
)
```

Function to draw the outcome using the expanded list generated by rewrite. See right for details.

```
(defun c:go ( )
 (command "erase" "all" "")
 (setvar "cmdecho" 0)
  (setq rules(list f)
       newrules'()
       p (list 0 0 0)
       count (getint "no of recursions")
       ang 90
       )
(setq   RHS '( f  L f l f l)
       LHS 'f
       axiom '(f)
       rules(rewrite RHS LHS axiom count)
       )
 (drawit rules )
(command "zoom" "e")
rules
)
```

The main program. If you have taken the trouble to type all this stuff in, then after loading, type 'GO' to run it.

The complete program for an infinite variety of recursive curves is very compact. Opposite is the complete program for generating an infinite number of 2D recursively defined drawings in AutoCAD.

In the text opposite, `(CAR thelist)` means the first symbol in the list. The function pulls off the first symbol, and then sends the rest of the list `(CDR thelist)` back to itself. See the discussion on page 67.

Converting the symbol string into a drawing

The EVAL function is called in the recursive function DRAWIT. This is passed the long list of symbols generated by the rewrite function and:

1. pulls off the front symbol in the list using CAR;
2. wraps it up as a list `(list (car thelist))`;
3. evaluates this;
4. passes the rest (all but the first) of the list back to itself `(CDR thelist)`.

There is a test to make sure we stop after the last symbol has been evaluated, i.e. takes each symbol in the generated LISP and works on the assumption that it is a function, e.g. it is a function called 'F', 'L' or 'R'.

We have already written these three functions (at the top of the code), so this assumption turns out to be justified, and so a cascade of calls to the line and rotation functions takes place automatically. There is no hidden code to translate these instructions – the total drawing is constructed by feeding the symbol string one by one to the EVAL function:

```
(eval (list(car thelist)))
```

Such is the power of EVAL, the trick introduced by the Turing machine at the beginning of this chapter where a computer is instructed to execute a symbol string (that it has itself constructed by executing some instructions) as though it were an instruction.

By altering the right-hand side in the program, you can generate a range of different curves, by altering the value of `ang`, the same curves take on a different set of shapes, etc.

Explicit representations of ineffable ideas

In Chapter 2 we considered the notion that two systems could be coupled together to produce an emergent consensual domain, in order to develop the imaginary idea that we are shoving things around when really all we are doing is redistributing some pixels painted behind the display.

Artificial life after intelligence

This section is concerned with showing that computer models of very primitive modes of perception help to illustrate the way that, by being embedded in the world, simple 'bodies' can develop a relationship with it which leads to the generation of abstract observations. Such observations as 'edge' or 'corner' can be expressed by the simplest computation. In effect this is a new description of space, not based on what we ourselves do, but on what very simple machines can do. As with Cellular Automata, L-systems, etc., this section also requires the proper definition of the observer.

Architecture, as has been said (to my knowledge by Bill Hillier at least), is about the creation of form and space for the occupation of people. The question arises how do we observe the space and form without simplistic models of perception based on the eye as a camera and the mind as a logic machine? In the *Phenomenology of Perception* (1962), Merleau-Ponty gathered the then current state (1945) of philosophical, intellectual rationalist and psychological ideas about consciousness and cognition, and set out a critique of these existing approaches based on 'being-in-the-world'. This allowed him to set out the idea that perception is an emergent outcome of the coupling together of the 'out there' and the 'in here', so that rather than the classical observer (me) and the world (as observed by God or science), we end up with a reflexive relation where the observer emerges from the interaction – the world observes itself, and we are part of it. To put it another way, the information traffic is not just 'eye > brain', but also 'brain > eye'; there is an equal two-way exchange of information between the brain and the eye. This approach to cognition has now become accepted and is referred to as the embedded mind paradigm, with much success in artificial life projects.

In all the other sections, we have looked at various abstractions of what doing a design might be, but here it may be more appropriate to take the bull by the horns and sink into that ultimate recursive regress, the self-creation of designs, and the last long stop of the discussion of design – intuition. In these models then, the absolute simplicity of the algorithm provides an observer free from the epistemological fog which Merleau-Ponty spent so long cutting apart.

It is the intention of this section to present intuition as an example of 'unconscious computation', and particularly to try and see enactive outcomes (described in what follows) as a model for intuition. Unconscious/intuitive behaviour is difficult to imagine, but a good example is that of 'blind sight' (Weiscrantz and Cowley, 1999), a situation where people loose their ability to see because of damage to their visual cortex (as opposed to their eyes and optical processing circuits). In some cases such people cannot see anything, and assume that they are blind. However, if asked to 'guess' the colour of a dot on the screen, they get it right 95% of the time. Similarly, given enough courage, such people can navigate across a room by guessing where the furniture is. What is happening is that they can 'see' in the sense that their eyes work ok, and low-level visual recognition is taking place normally, but because of the damage to the back of the brain they do not know that they can see, as the scene is not projected onto that curious internal screen that we assume is what consciousness is. Such a person can relearn to navigate and so on by tuning in to the actual processing going on, listening out for 'hunches', 'vague feelings' in fact (a bold jump this), going by their intuitions.

The word creative/creativity has not been used in any section of this book quite deliberately, as the author finds such discussions, especially when conducted by computer scientists, circular and pointless. However, it is interesting to note that those architectural educators who encourage intuition in design also make a point of saying that we cannot know how the design was arrived at, that creativity is something that cannot be taught, but only nurtured and hopefully recognised.

In this section the idea of the structural coupling of systems is explored as a way of trying to illustrate the idea of intuition as a computation. When a design emerges as a result of structural coupling between two systems, we can be very clear about the individual systems and how they are defined, but the point is the actual outcome is something in between, which is not actually described at all. Another way of putting it would be that the systems generate a meta system at a higher level of abstraction, which is why this view can be a good model for the idea that we can explain what design is.

Winograd's SHRDLU taken from Margaret Boden *Artificial Intelligence and Natural Man* (MIT Press). SHRDLU, by Terry Winograd, was written in PLANNER, which, in turn, was derived from LISP.

SHRDLU is named after the second column of type keys on a Linotype machine – the full name is, of course, ETAOIN SHRDLU, the letters of the alphabet in descending order of occurrence in English.

To Michael Frayn's delight, many newspapers contained references to both these words, as Linotype operators would run their fingers down the keyboard to flag up a typo to the printers (there is no undo on a hot metal machine) and if they were missed would appear on the page.

Nowadays it would be QWERTYUIOP, of course.

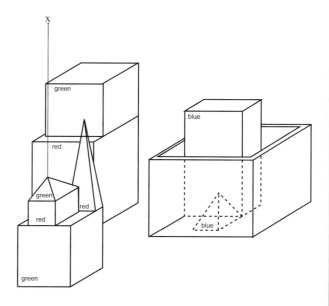

20   *Conversation with SHRDLU*

FIGURE 6.4
"Does the shortest thing the tallest pyramid supports support anything green?"

Source: Adapted from Terry Winograd. *Procedures as Representations for Data in a Computer Program for Understanding Natural* language. (Ph.D. thesis). (Cambridge, Mass.) AI-TR-17. MIT AI Lab), p.49. Reprinted by permission.

25. *why?*
    The system remembers immediately previous sentences to understand questions like this and the following ones
        TO GET RID OF IT.
    By keeping track of selected parts of the original subgoal tree, the system has some understanding of it's own motives.

26. *why did you do that?*
        TO CLEAN OFF THE RED CUBE
        "That" refers to the action mentioned in the answer.

27. *why did you clear off that cube?*
        Here, "that" means the one just referred to.
        TO PUT IT ON A LARGE GREEN CUBE

28. *why did you do that?*
        TO STACK UP THE RED CUBE, A LARGE RED BLOCK AND A LARGE GREEN CUBE.

The embedded/embodied idea

Behind the general notions of cognition lie the fundamental idea that all structures of understanding (in perceptive beings) or structures of organisation (in things) depend on being embedded in a rich environment of stimuli and action. This is much stronger than saying that we learn by doing, and in particular insists on blurring the distinction between the perceiver and the perceived. It is an interesting observation to note that only mobile life forms evolve brains/consciousness, and that just to prove the point certain life forms that begin life mobile and then take root, immediately eat their brains once they stop moving (this well-known behaviour is reported in the case of the sea squirt).

In the first attempts at modelling cognitive behaviour (famously Terry Winograd's SHRDLU blocks world system), the environment was modelled as a problem in logic, with solutions having to be computed by a fixed series of logical steps (Take the red box off the blue one? First move the green box off the red one, then move the red one, etc., etc., ect.). SHRDLU worked well in this tightly defined virtual blocks world, but to expand its repertoire would have required another five-year programming effort for each new task.

Nowadays robots do not get fed strict logical rules, but are placed in a real physical environment and given a chance to bump into things. Because their brains are neural nets they can slowly evolve behaviours and become general purpose walkers, lifters, etc. The maze is as important as the rat, as it were. The embedded idea is that you must have a rich environment for any emergent intelligence to happen, and the embodied idea is that you must have a good set of perceptive mechanisms so as to be able to interact with the environment. Generally, the complexity of the outcome (how well the robot navigates, how good a fit the design is to its intended task) is not dependent on the complexity of its internal wiring, but on the complexity of its environment and the possible complexity of its interactions via its perceptive mechanisms. The encouraging thing we learn from nature is to hitch a ride on the complexity of the rest of the environment and to just adapt simple designs to be 'good enough', rather than engineer brand new systems from scratch every time.

The phototropic robot

A good example of the emergence of a consensual domain can be found in very simple perceptive machines. The description that follows describes a set of experiments carried out by Pablo Miranda Carranza at the University of East London in 1999–2000. To begin with, a simple turtle was built, based on the reflex behaviour by which moths and other insects are attracted to light, known as 'positive phototropism'. In this mechanism the two halves of the motoric capacity of an insect are alternatively exited and inhibited, depending on the side from which they perceive a strong source of light, having the effect of steering the insect towards the light source. The automaton consisted of two light sensors each connected to threshold devices and these to two electric motors (one in each side of the body). The device is thus made of two completely independent effectors (sensory-motor units). The automaton exhibits different behaviours depending on the configuration of its parts, in particular changing the position of the light sensors with respect to the rest of the components, and causes the machine to wander in different ways through a rectangular white area: sometimes groping the edges, at other times covering the whole surface, at yet other times stopping at the corners. Although all operations involved in the 'computation' of this automaton were elementary, the organisation of these operations allows us to appreciate a principle of considerable complexity such as the computation of abstracts.

The system built is an example of a much-used design, available for instance from Lego, programmable in NetLogo. Pablo Miranda's robot uses light and dark on the ground for steering.

Thus, when a light sensitive robot crawls round the edge of a piece of white paper, leaving a trail behind it, we can think of the mark drawn on the paper as a record of the outcome of the coupling between the sensory bits and the moving bits of the robot. If the robot manages to stay on the paper, then we can say that the robot's coupling between these two parts is successful, and the trail drawn is the robot's 'understanding' of the edge (i.e. the trace of a successful trajectory in the problem space). You can alter the trail by changing the position of the eyes, or the wheels or the circuit between them, in which case the outcome may be more or less successful, looser or tighter curves, etc.

Gray Walter – 'imitation of life'

W. Gray Walter's original 1948 robots 'Elmer and Elsie' (which he dubbed *M. Speculatrix* in cod Latin in a paper whose title – *The Imitation of Life* (Walter, 1951) – refers obliquely to St Thomas Aquinas) were equipped with two (thermionic) valves, a motion sensor, and a photo sensitive cell. They tended to move towards the light, but away from objects that they bumped into (and bright lights), they also kept track of their battery charge and, as this dropped, the relative strength of the light tropism increased, guiding them back to the battery charger (which had a light on top). He noted the emergence of 'intelligent' behaviour with these simple feedback loops (all quotes taken from *The Imitation of Life* (1950)):

> 'If there is a single light source, the machine circles around it in a complex path of advance and withdrawal; if there is another light farther away, the machine will visit first one and then the other and will continually stroll back and forth between the two. In this way it neatly solves the dilemma of Buridan's ass, which the scholastic philosophers said would die of starvation between two barrels of hay if it did not possess a transcendental free will.'

The robots behave in a rational manner when dealing with static lights, but Walter also experimented with moving lights by putting a candle on both Elmer and Elsie's carapaces. In this way both robots are tracking a moving target, and become bound up in a double feedback loop where each one effects the other and so on. Walter observed:

'Two creatures of this type meeting face to face are affected in a similar but again distinctive manner. Each, attracted by the light the other carries, extinguishes its own source of attraction, so the two systems become involved in a mutual oscillation, leading finally to a stately retreat.'

As he wrote:

'Crude though they are, they give an eerie impression of purposefulness, independence and spontaneity.'

The point here is that, as a human watches a robot, there are two observations going on – what the human observer thinks is going on, and what the robots think is going on (or if you want to be pedantic, what they have been programmed to do). Grey Walter, when looking at the robots with candles on their backs, thought that they were behaving in a complex way with some purpose other than the programmed looking for food/light. However, Elmer and Elsie were just doing the same thing as usual; their programs had not changed so as observers of light they were just the same.

Walter was witnessing something that few people had at that time, an appearance of purposeful behaviour that, in this case, was entirely explicable (knowable) in that he himself had built the machines – he knew down to the last bolt and electron what was going on. Walter could define all of the components of the system – the first time this had ever been possible in an unbroken chain of engineering from the phenomenon down to the code/hardware/physics of the life forms in front of him.

This hierarchy of observations occurs for us in the world as well of course, and in particular it is interesting to note that we, as observers, are naturally given to imputing a kind of teleology and intelligence to the activity of creatures whose internal states we cannot observe easily.

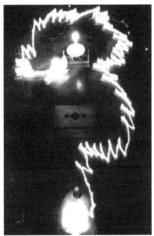

Pictures taken of Elmer and Elsie by Walter – these and other images are held in the Walter archive at the University of the West of England, Bristol, in memory of that institution's most pioneering engineer. 'Elmer and Elsie' was the title of a musical popular in the 1930s.

Spiders' webs after the rain, Montauban, 2007

Interlude: the spider as a machine

This Artificial Life parable of the natural world is offered as a reflection on the idea that the behaviour of a spider could be entirely explicable given the increasingly encouraging developments in neural networks and robotics. I suppose it is a reverse Elmer and Elsie moment, that of seeing the machine in the life as opposed to seeing the life in the machine. Instead of Walter's observing the apparently 'life-like' emergent outcomes of the structural coupling of two indubitably simple machines, this is an example of observing 'machine-like' behaviour in what was indubitably alive.

> 'When we rejoined the car in the ferry garage, I noticed that during the course of the voyage, a fairly large spider had built a web between the pipes and flanges of the upper deck and our car aerial. In getting into the car we broke the web, and the neat polygon lost one of its vertices. Thus the tight surface was collapsed and half was swinging loosely.
>
> At that point one would usually drive off and never give it a thought, but there was a long wait . . .
>
> I started staring out of the sunroof. At some point the spider appeared, and seemed fairly excited, presumably because she thought dinner big time had arrived, but eventually it sunk in that there was only damage and no food. It seemed as if maintenance was the only option, but I must say I did not give her much chance of repairing the web. Looking at the spider moving about, it was impossible not to be reminded of the slightly random jerkiness of maze-solving robots, which nevertheless reach their goal. The Artificial Life like thing was the way not all moves were successful, but generally good moves began to outnumber bad ones. Sentient beings try never to make mistakes; most of the time the spider battled on looking like someone trying to strap down the cargo on a storm-tossed boat.
>
> Eventually it was possible to recognise certain sets of moves. There were a number of passes over the main holding points, and what looked like an attempt at a quick fix (if I just pull this bit here it will all come together), but nothing much happened. Then, after what seemed like ages, she started building a sort of scaffolding weblet, and finally hooking the dangly bits and gluing them onto the now slightly stiffer remaining bit. Eventually she managed to repair the web, although admittedly a rather misshapen version of the original.
>
> How complex would a machine have to be to do this? The answer is, of course, as complex as a spider needing to repair a web. It took evolution 380 million years.
>
> When we drove off we probably destroyed the spider's web.
>
> But a spider is just one of billions of self-replicating spider machines, so that's alright.'
>
> (Observations during a ferry ride,
> Dun Laoghaire to Milford Haven, New Year, 2000)

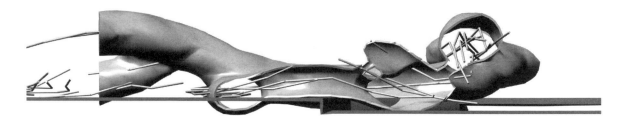

Agent trails wrapped in isosurfaces
(Miranda, Swarm Intelligence, 2000)

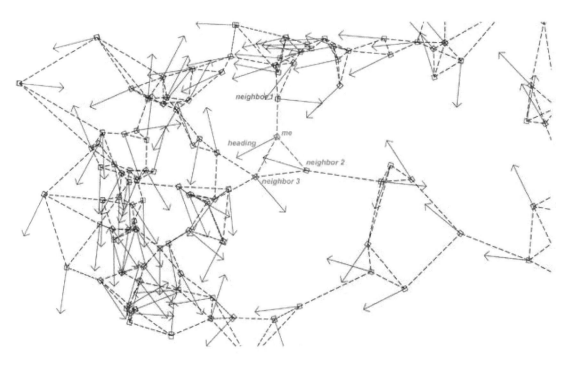

Agent trails diagram of flocking behaviour
(Miranda, Swarm Intelligence, 2000)

Swarm: embodiment and description of form

How then can these ideas about embedded/embodied perceivers and emergent consensual domains be applied to the notion of architectural design? One way would be to construct some very simple embodied perceivers and to let them loose in an environment.

The sensori-motor experiments described earlier were therefore replicated in virtuo using Craig Reynolds' flocking algorithm, with a flock of swarming 'boids' (the word 'bird' in a New Jersey accent – some American joke about the unreality of that suburb) inhabiting an environment modelled to represent the confluence of the lea valley and the Thames. Here we have a swarm system, and the structural coupling is emergent from the way the boids change their flight paths as a consequence of their environment. The swarm consists of a number of individuals who are normally in a reflexive relation one to another – chasing each other's tails as it were – and will show emergent structure as groups of boids flock together into aggregates then break up and reform, etc. The emergent swarm is visible as a structured and controlled meta behaviour which is not directly programmed into the behaviour of each individual, but arises by the simultaneous actions of the boids. This emergent behaviour will occur anyway, with the boid's environment consisting of all the other boids (and vice versa), but if the flock is immersed in a geometrical environment as well, then obstacle avoidance will perturb the individual trajectories of boids, and those will, in turn, perturb other boids and so on. Thus the site geometry perturbs the flock, resulting in a globally observable structure which is different from the unperturbed example.

The algorithm

Each agent has direct access to the whole scene's geometric description, but reacts only to flockmates within a certain small radius of itself. The basic flocking model consists of three simple steering behaviours:

- *Separation* – gives an agent the ability to maintain a certain separation distance from others nearby. This prevents agents from crowding too closely together, allowing them to scan a wider area. To compute steering for separation, first a search is made to find other individuals within the specified neighbourhood. For each nearby agent, a repulsive force is computed by subtracting the positions of our agent and the nearby ones and normalising

the resultant vector. These repulsive forces for each nearby character are summed together to produce the overall steering force.

- *Cohesion* – gives an agent the ability to cohere (approach and form a group) with other nearby agents. Steering for cohesion can be computed by finding all agents in the local neighbourhood and computing the 'average position' of the nearby agents. The steering force is then applied in the direction of that 'average position'.
- *Alignment* – gives an agent the ability to align itself with other nearby characters. Steering for alignment can be computed by finding all agents in the local neighbourhood and averaging together the 'heading' vectors of the nearby agents. This steering will tend to turn our agent so it is aligned with its neighbours.

Obstacle avoidance

In addition, the behavioural model includes predictive obstacle avoidance. Obstacle avoidance allows the agents to fly through simulated environments while dodging static objects. The behaviour implemented can deal with arbitrary shapes and allows the agents to navigate close to the obstacle's surface. The agents test the space ahead of them with probe points.

Results

In this experiment, as a result of the way the collision detection algorithm worked (slowly rectifying the heading of the agent until it found a collision-free trajectory), the individual agents had a tendency to align with the surfaces of the geometric model of the site. This ended in the emergence of the 'smoothest' trajectory on the environment, which, in the case of the test model of a site, were the meanders of the River Lea. The swarm is able to discriminate the edges of a long wide curvy groove, that is, the geometric form of the river, from any other information such as buildings or building groups or infrastructures.

This first experiment was interesting from the point of view of defining parallelisms with the first automaton and studying the emergence of the collective behaviour of the swarm, and also its ability for 'describing' form. The point is that the boids would have formed patterns anyway, but the ones we see here are the result of this behaviour being perturbed by the site model and, in particular, the detailed way in which the flocking behaviour has this unintended consequence of 'finding' long slow curves in its environment.

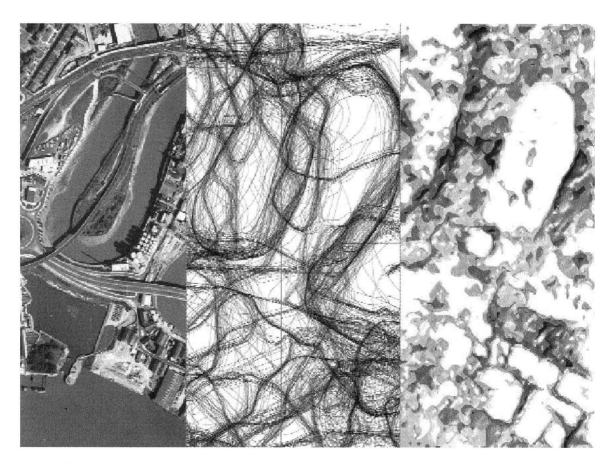

Agents in the Lea Valley
(Miranda, Swarm Intelligence. 2000)

Why did the agents/boids describe the river rather than the buildings? A couple of possibilities offer themselves:

- Resolution – the swarm is too coarse a perceptor to allow it to 'see' the buildings enough times to make an appreciable effect on its behaviour.
- Geometry – perhaps the curve (made by fluid dynamics – it is a river after all) is easier to recognise because of its emergent form giving it an innately more readable description.

In Chapter 1 the general notion of distributed representation was introduced, and in Chapter 2 the different levels of observation were mentioned. The deeper and more interesting questions –'What is form?' and 'What is space?' – have to be addressed in order to ground the practical experiments. The aim of the work described above is to look at how form and space can be generated using a model which corresponds as closely as possible to the idea of the embodied mind, without relying on 'hand of God' short cuts. In the end it comes down to being very precise about the status of the observer, and by seeing a hierarchy of observations, just as in the case of the multiple order observations in the case of the Cellular Automata described earlier, from local to global.

chapter four

Evolving the text – being even lazier

Over the last 50 years the people who write the code have doggedly spent most of their time avoiding work. The development of general solutions to particular problems has led to reusable libraries of code so that no one needs to ever write a window from scratch or laboriously render the text – someone somewhere will have done this already, so just get it and use it. The whole history of computing is a slow ascent from mind-bendingly tedious machine code, where every procedure must be written anew for a new machine, to portable languages like Java, which are designed to run on an imaginary computer. The task is to squeeze out the essence of the difference into one tiny package which needs to be written for a new situation, and then to balance the heap of ready written stuff on top of it.

But there is one possibility that has always intrigued the lazy coders, what if we could get the computer to write the code for us – so we just write one program which evolves a program, and then we can all go back to sleep!

This approach is usually labelled Genetic Programming (GP) and is a development of evolutionary algorithms. Before looking at GP, therefore, it will be necessary to take a look at the underlying principles of evolutionary algorithms.

The purpose of the previous chapter on L-systems is to set the scene for the next layer of abstraction, where the codes are generated by meta-grammars rather then set out by hand. This takes the idea of symbolic notation beyond the simple generative experiment, towards the derivation of a set of automatically defined theorems (lemmas) which form part of the structure of the formal language. The general mechanics of evolutionary algorithms are discussed first, in the context of a simple morphological Genetic Algorithm, and then the concepts of crossover, mutation and breeding are shown in the contexts of formal systems using GP.

Morphological evolutionary algorithms

The following discussion sets out the basic way that you can program a simple evolutionary algorithm to optimise a very basic geometrical problem. It covers all the main components of the task, and can be used as a template for other evolutionary algorithms. The examples show how, in the first place, natural selection can be used to automatically design a 'fit' object, and, in the second place, the example of artificial selection, where the user selects the fittest objects by visual inspection. In either example we can observe Machine Learning, where the program slowly adapts the design to suit the fitness function. Where the fitness function is explicit (referred to as the objective function), then the whole process is closed, and the learning takes place by the machine on its own. Where the fitness function is user-defined, then the learning process has to include the human operator, so that the feedback loop extends outside the machine, through the human (whose eyes and brain are used to select the fittest objects) and back again. In this way both the machine and the user are training each other, with the user being presented with examples which s/he may not have contemplated before, so that the walk through the search space is continuously unfolding as a result of previous choices. Interacting with such a learning machine is at first quite an eerie experience, as the computer seems to adapt itself to your unspoken preferences (an idea of 'spikeyness' in the case of the artificial selection, for example). These mechanisms are also explored in the GP examples as well, where more complex architectural objects are discussed.

The main thing to be decided before embarking on an evolutionary algorithm is how the geometry to be evolved is to be represented in the computer. What procedures need to be written to generate the form, and what parameters do these procedures need? Together this is referred to as the embryology, or

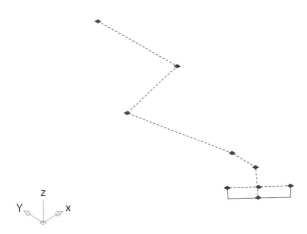

A polyline of six vertices plus a profile to sweep along the line

Six vertices of two coordinates each = 12 parameters
Width and height of rectangle = 2

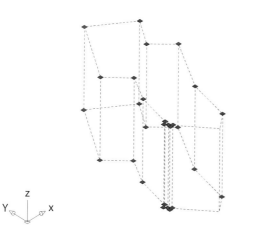

Result of sweeping the rectangle along the line

Total parameters 12+ 2 = 14

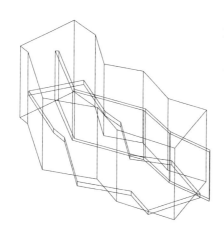

Doing this four times

14 times 4 = 56

The Body Plan for this object
and a field of examples

Body Plan, that is to say the repertoire of form-creating methods and their various numbers. The same numbers fed to two different sets of form creating methods will result in two different outcomes. This is not to be confused with giving the same method two different sets of numbers. The embryology, in these simple examples, is not under evolutionary pressure, it is outside the system and does not change. In the later GP examples, the Body Plan is, to some extent, under selection pressure, especially in the case of Helen Jackson's structural outcomes using L-systems (Jackson and Coates, 1999). In 1988, Richard Dawkins set out the main aspects of the importance of the Body Plan in his paper 'The Evolution of Evolvability'. Essentially there are two different things going on in an evolutionary algorithm:

1. The process of development – how the code of the genes is expressed to form the phenotype. The phenotype in this case is a set of 3D volumes consisting of four extruded polylines which together make up the object visible in the illustrations on the facing page.
2. The process of genetics – how the gene code is modified and adapted in the process of evolution. The genotype in this case is a string representing 56 numbers – four sets of 14 which are decoded into the parameters for the four extruded polylines (explained below). These together constitute the genetic material – the chromosome.

In the natural world such things are also capable of evolution, though at a different level as it were. At the highest level of abstraction are the fundamental constructions of DNA, with its four-letter code A C G T. Although it is theoretically possible to conceive of forms of life that are based on different atoms and chemistry, none has been found on this planet, and it is assumed that all evolution has started from the same primitive cells. In artificial evolution we can choose the coding scheme to suit the problem.

Encoding the Body Plan – the polyline example
The polyline example was developed by an MSc student some time ago. We all liked it because it displayed a kind of architectural quality yet was sufficiently simple to be encoded easily. The task of encoding in this case is to define:

1. a profile that is defined as a polyline of six vertices;
2. the width and height of the profile to be swept along the polyline; and
3. *this happens four times*.

After choosing a scheme for the phenotype and the genotype, these individual parameters must be coded into binary numbers. So we end up with 56 pieces of data that we have to encode. Each piece we will designate a '*word*'.

A word is a binary string that encodes one parameter. A parameter is a value we use to build the model. In this case, the word is five binary numbers long, so the gene will be in total 56 x 5 = 280 bits long.

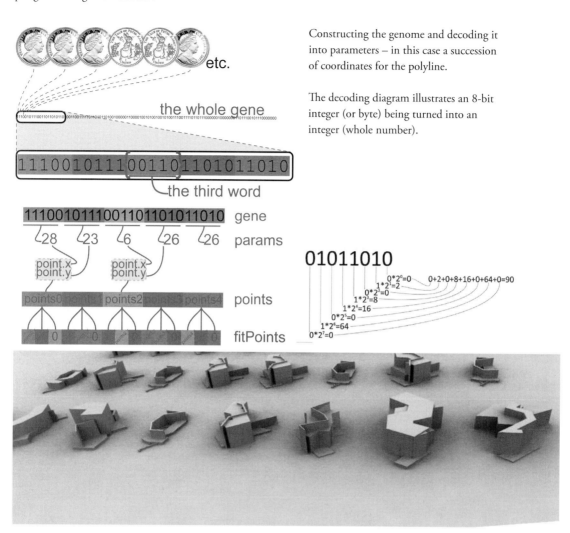

Constructing the genome and decoding it into parameters – in this case a succession of coordinates for the polyline.

The decoding diagram illustrates an 8-bit integer (or byte) being turned into an integer (whole number).

etc.

the whole gene

the third word

11100101110011011101011010 gene

28 23 6 26 26 params

point.x
point.y   point.x
               point.y

points0 points1 points2 points3 points4 points

0   0   0   0   0 fitPoints

01011010

$0*2^0=0$ $0+2+0+8+16+0+64+0=90$
$1*2^1=2$
$0*2^2=0$
$1*2^3=8$
$1*2^4=16$
$0*2^5=0$
$1*2^6=64$
$0*2^7=0$

Initial population of phenotypes generated from the
56 parameters per individual – front row

The next step is to create the initial population of individuals by generating a string of 280 binary numbers for each individual, essentially flipping a coin 280 times to give heads or tails – 1 or 0. These strings are then decoded into 56 numbers which provides the array of numbers needed to draw one individual. At this stage the population is a very diverse bunch of characters with different thicknesses, wigglyness, height and so on (written in pseudocode, i.e. not a real computer language):

```
to make a gene

  gene = empty

  For each character in the gene

  random = a random number between 0 an 1

  If random is less than 0.5 then
     put "1" into gene
  Else
     put "0" into gene
  End If

  next character

End make a gene
```

Fitness function

Once this initial population exists, we can test each member to see how well it performed. Of course in this initial try they will all perform pretty badly. The fitness function is the last piece of the jigsaw, and is the most tricky to design. Too harsh a fitness test may result in the Genetic Algorithm never getting off the ground as it were; too relaxed and the Genetic Algorithm never settles down to an optimum. In this case the fitness function is designed to reward individuals that have a high volume, but a small footprint (the developer's Manhattan function, as it were), as though they were competing for rent in a city. Thus we need a reward (for volume), but also a punishment (for over large footprint).

However, the simple comparing of volume and footprint to give a score has to be modified because the computer cheats (or rather it takes the fitness function literally). By just rewarding a polyline with the volume less the footprint, it turns out that very large volumes with big footprints do better than larger volumes with less footprint, so the fitness function has to be:

fitness = volume x rewardfactor – footprint x punishfactor

punish = this individual's footprint x 10
reward = this individual's volume x 1

this individual's fitness = reward – punish

in order to punish profligate footprint growing and reward volume. The factors are to allow for adjustments in case the values for either component are in need of some scaling. In this case the reward factor is 1 and the punish factor is 10.

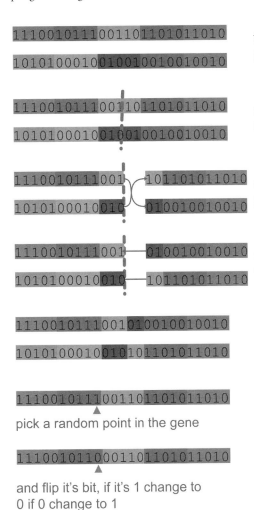

take the two
parent genes

choose a random point
along the gene string

split the gene into two
parts and swap over

stick them back together
to form two new genes

pick a random point in the gene

and flip it's bit, if it's 1 change to
0 if 0 change to 1

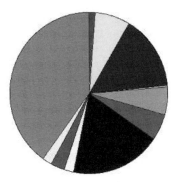

Goldberg's weighted roulette
wheel – the size of the segment is
proportional to the fitness of an
individual

Goldberg's weighted roulette wheel

So now that we have the population assessed and each phenotype has a score, we now have to select the members of the population to breed from. Crudely put, we need to select the fittest individuals to pass their genes on to the next generation. However, especially in the early generations, the guys with the best scores may well be pretty bad (in the land of the blind, the one eyed man is king, etc.), so David Goldberg designed the weighted roulette wheel so that, while high scoring individuals are more likely to be chosen, there is always a residual chance that the others get a look-in too.

The diagram opposite illustrates the idea. The different shaded slices of the pie are sized relative to the fitness of each individual, rather than being all the same size (as on a normal roulette wheel). The chances of the ball landing on a particular slice are therefore proportional to the fitness of each individual. The wheel is spun twice for each breeding pair, whose genes are mixed by the operation of crossover.

Crossover

Although John Holland (one of the early pioneers of Genetic Algorithm) has published a number of papers in an attempt to explain why crossover works, the fact is that it was adopted simply because this is the way that nature does it, and it works! The mechanism is very simple, two chromosomes are lined up next to each other and cut across somewhere along their length. The two cut ends are then swapped and glued back onto the opposite end of the chromosome.

The key thing is that, because the parameters to the morphology growing process are coded in binary and then stuck together as a continuous strip, the crossover point is usually in the middle of an allele (word), thus producing a completely different number from the original. If the parameter values were not coded, but simply held as 14 inviolate numbers, then all we would be doing is shuffling the pack. This way we not only shuffle the pack, but also create brand new cards as it were.

Mutation

While the new chromosomes are being copied, a very small chance is given to make a mistake, substituting a 1 for a 0 or vice-versa as the children are set up. This allows for further variety, and is included for the sake of avoiding settling down too soon to sub-optimal outcomes, and again because Darwin said that random mutations were part of evolution.

Evolution

After the weighted roulette wheel has been spun eight times we have a new population, which is drawn, tested and selected again, and so on until the number of generations is completed.

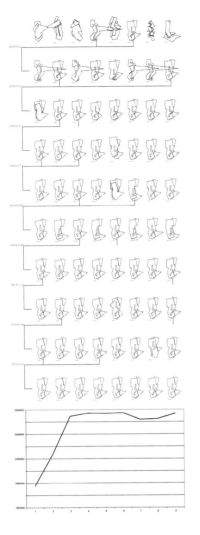

Two different runs of the developer's fitness function

fitness = volume – (footprint x 10)

Top row – the initial random population. As the generations progress, the total fitness of the population grows – quickly at first, then levels off. The individuals begin quickly to resemble one another, i.e. the amount of genetic variation drops. The two runs show that, depending where you start in the fitness landscape, you arrive at different results. (The left-hand series never quite reaches the fitness of the right-hand series.)

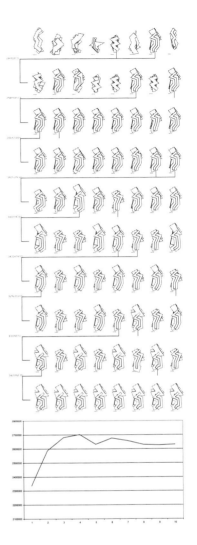

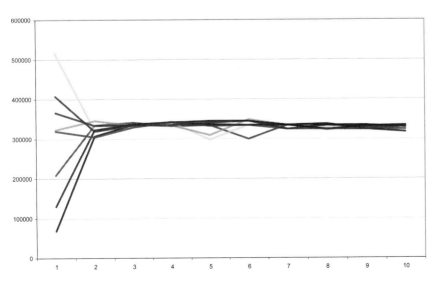

The eight individual's fitnesses graphed together. The crossover operation enforces homogeneity in the gene pool leading to a collective fitness somewhere below the best result in the first generation

Natural verus artificial selection

Natural selection, being a purely automatic process, defers all architectural decisions to the fitness function, which in this 'toy' example is necessarily simple. It is the code that represents the intentions of the designer, and to extend and develop the design we have, of course, to think about how to come up with more interesting body plans. With all evolutionary algorithms the fundamental notion is to see design as a search process in a space (the search space) that is defined by the ways in which the parameters can be combined. With 56 parameters one might say that the size of this space is all the ways to combine 56 numbers, which is a fairly huge number anyway, but because of the way individual numbers can themselves be mutated and changed by crossover, the search space goes up to 54 x 5 = 270. Now factorial 270 (270!) is an absolutely huge number (in fact while the factorial of 56 is given as 7.109985878048632e+74 (7.1 with 74 zeros after it), the factorial of 270 is given as infinite. Even if we severely restrict the number of possible permutations or combinations, the search space is such that an exhaustive enumeration would take longer than the history of the universe on any current computer. The main justification for the evolutionary algorithm is that it cuts down the time needed to search this space, by chasing 'likely monsters' (as Dawkins calls them) and by quickly discarding unlikely combinations early on. It is instructive to contemplate how many different evolutionary experiments have been abandoned over the course of the last few billion years, but from our perspective we are certainly the lucky ones, as the survivors of the survivors of the survivors of the survivors . . .

It is also relevant that the initial choice of Body Plan has a big effect on the likelihood of evolving anything useful in finite time, and in fact the definition of a useful Body Plan is as much a design decision as any employed by a hand craft approach to design.

With the appropriate Body Plan and fitness function we can (almost too) quickly arrive at a particular design in less that 10 generations in the examples shown. Given the initial random population of the evolution, with this small a population, once the unselected individuals have been removed from the gene pool, there is little variation left with which to play. Nevertheless, you can run the process many times with different random initial populations, and the interaction between the human observer and the machine is quite a nice example of what one might term 'Computer Aided Design'.

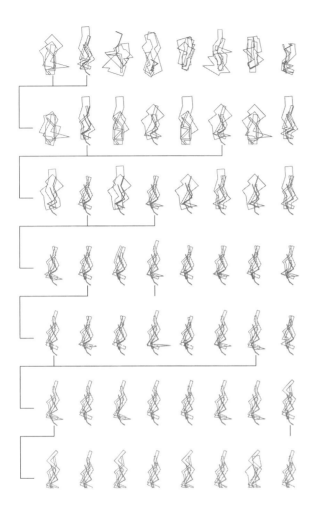

History of artificial selection – the chosen individuals for breeding are indicated in the diagram left. Initial population at the top, generations generated downwards. The initial population at the top consists of a fairly wide range of phenotypes, which were then selected by natural selection based on the footprint/volume formula described on the previous page. The isometric image shows the detailed morphology that has emerged from this selection process which provides a kind of stylistic trajectory of family of forms which are kicked off by the initial random settings of the first family of individuals. By the last generation the differences are very small – almost as though we are watching the development of an ever more nuanced approach to design by developing this particular typology.

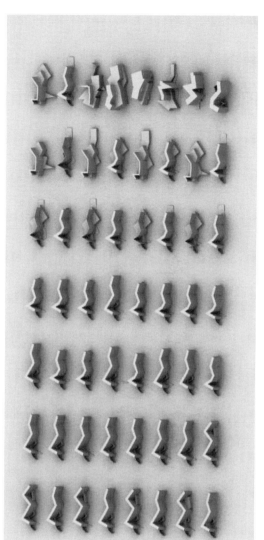

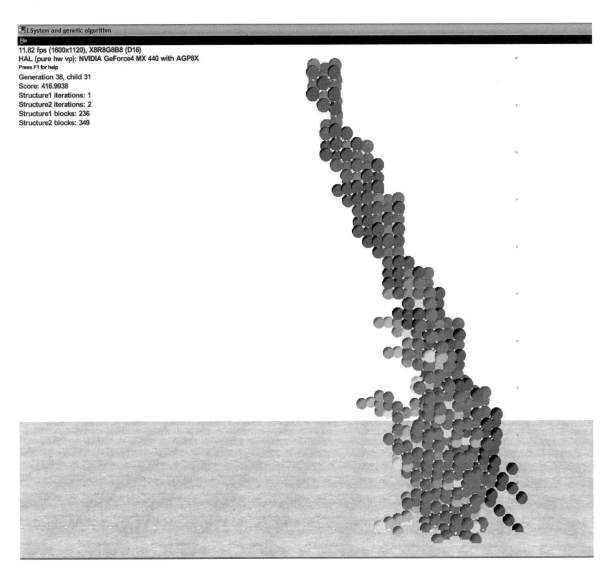

L System and genetic algorithm
File
11.82 fps (1600x1120), X8R8G8B8 (D16)
HAL (pure hw vp): NVIDIA GeForce4 MX 440 with AGP8X
Press F1 for help
Generation 38, child 31
Score: 416.9938
Structure1 iterations: 1
Structure2 iterations: 2
Structure1 blocks: 236
Structure2 blocks: 349

Co-evolutionary GP L-system structure using two systems
both of whose fitness function depends on supporting
the other by means of a load model designed by Galasyn.
Reproduced by permission of Jim Galasyn

Evolving what ?

The great failing of these kinds of algorithms is that, while they are good at exploring the design space defined by their parameters, they cannot transcend them. For example, Genetic Algorithms can be used to design the hull of a sailing boat, with parameters for curvature and fitness function of minimising drag, but such an algorithm would never come up with a catamaran.

To extend the search space in that way would mean more than just extending the number of parameters to the morphological procedures, but rewriting the procedures themselves. This is where GP comes in, because in GP the morphological procedures are actually defined as a set of lower level functions which themselves can be rearranged by evolution to become new procedures.

Genetic Programming

Genetic Programming (Koza, 1992) is a method of adapting the principles of evolutionary programming (such as Genetic Algorithms, classifier systems and simulated annealing) to the evolution of programs. Koza's contribution was to propose that rather than representing genetic material (the allelles) of a phenotype as a coded string, they could be represented as a branching tree structure of nested functions. In the original example the functions were arithmetic and mathematical, and the genotype was evaluated to make a numerical result.

These examples are introduced as a development of the LISP L-systems discussion of the previous chapter. In that discussion we looked at the way the code of the algorithm written in LISP (a text) could be used to generate another set of instructions by recursively expanding the code using the replacement of symbols by longer strings to produce the list of L-system function names (a further bit of text) which in turn drive the drawing functions to produce the drawing.

If the simple execution of code could be described as a first order operation (TEXT > OUTPUT), then the L-system can be seen as a second order operation (TEXT > OUTPUT > TEXT > OUTPUT). In the case of GP, we have a third-order operation where:

1. the text of the Genetic Algorithm works like the standard L-system, producing codes that produce phenotypes;
2. but unlike the simple Genetic Algorithm described above, it also exposes these codes to selection pressure so that the Body Plan and, therefore, the developmental process also changes as the run continues; and
3. the ouput from these evolved developmental processes then creates the phenotype, itself under evolutionary pressure.

In this way the evolutionary process is not just exploring the space of possible designs, given a particular Body Plan (like the polyline example on page 103), but exploring the space of all Body Plans given the fundamental components of the ur-Body Plan as it were.

The basic branching system is set out as follows

```
(f (p- y+ f)(p+ y- f)(r+ y+ f)(r- y- f))
       1        2        3        4
```

This means

  go forward f)

then the four sets of brackets set out above define the rotations of the coordinate system needed to draw the four branches in the right direction. After three generations of selecting for larger trees, it has become:

```
(F (P- Y+ F) (F (P- Y+ F) (F (F (P- Y+ F)
(P+ Y- F) (R+ Y+ F) (R- Y- F)) (P+ Y- F)
(R+ Y+ F) (R- Y- F)) (R+ Y+ F) (R- Y- F))
(R+ Y+ F) (R- Y-F))
```

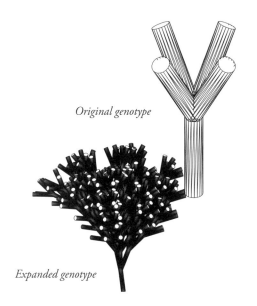

Original genotype

Expanded genotype

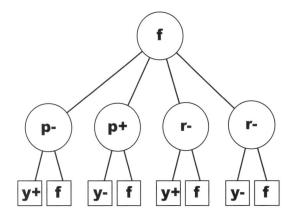

The symbol list is read by the GP system as a series of nestec function where each set of brackets is taken to be a separate sub-tree. In the diagram on the left the circles represent the first thing after a bracket, the boxes the rest of the list up to the next matching bracket.

Below four generations using artificial selection to breed large trees.

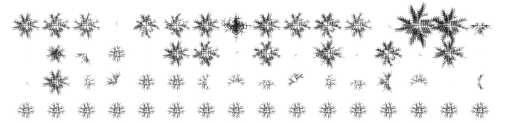

**Crossover and mutation in Genetic Programmimg –
an example using 3D branching L-system**

We looked at L-systems in the previous chapter.
The example was two dimensional and essentially
drew a continuous line so as to keep it simple. As an
introduction to the ideas of GP (evolving a text that in
turn draws the genotype), we extend this into 3D. To do
this we need to extend the original functions L (left) and
R (right) so that we can do the turtle drawing in three
axes. This can be simply achieved by using the AutoCAD
UCS as before, in the x and y axes. The z axis rotation is
now renamed YAW positive and negative, rather than L
and R. Notice that we are keeping to the turtle drawing
convention of always drawing a line from 0,0,0 to 0,0,1,
so that the function is always the same, but rotating the
universe as in 2D.

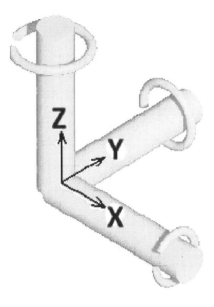

Roll allows rotation about the x axis clockwise or
counterclockwise:

```
(defun r+ ()
  (command "ucs" "x" ang)
(defun r- ()
  (command "ucs" "x" (- ang))
Pich about the Y
(defun p+ ()
  (command "ucs" "y" ang)
(defun p- ()
  (command "ucs" "y" (- ang))
Yaw about the Z (same as rotate in 2d)
(defun y+ ()
  (command "ucs" "z" ang)
(defun y- ()
  (command "ucs" "z" (- ang))
F is now a cylinder rather than a line
  whose length is H and radius is rad
(defun F ( / tp)
  (command "_cylinder" rad '(0 0 0) h)
  (setq tp (list 0 0 h))
  (command "ucs" "o" tp)
```

As in the 2D example we move the origin of the
universe to the end of the cylinder once we have drawn
it.

The genome in GP is held in a different way to the
Genetic Algorithm. Rather than a linear string of digits,
traditionally in GP it is defined as a function tree. Also in
this L-system we are using a branching system (referred
to in the literature as a bracketed system because the
place where the code needs to branch is marked by a
bracket). When a left-hand bracket is encountered in the
list the program has to:

1. remember where it is in 3D;
2. draw the branch; and
3. move to the end of the branch.

When a right-hand bracket is encountered, the program
leaves the position it has reached and returns to the
place it remembered in step 1.

Before crossover
Individual A

Individual B

After crossover
Individual C

Individual D

Crossover in GP consists of snipping a random sub-tree off two individual's function trees and swapping them. Unlike Genetic Algorithms, the result of breeding like this is that descendants can have more (or less) functions than their parents.

How the genome evolves

In this case instead of a random first population, we use the simple tree to start with. After each generation two of the the fittest phenotypes are chosen either by the user or by natural selection as described in the polyline example on page 103 in the description of a Genetic Algorithm. As we saw earlier, their genes must be combined to produce two new individuals who will hopefully be fitter than their parents. To do this the program first of all works out how many functions there are in the genome. Then it calcultes a random choice of sub-tree to select. It then trundles down the tree, keeping count of where it has got to until reaching the chosen sub-tree and essentially prunes it and all dependent sub-sub-trees.

It does this for the other chosen parent, so now it has two sub-trees to play with (highlighted in the diagram on the left). These two sub-trees are then swapped over and grafted back on the other parent's main rooting stock as it were.

Mutation works in much the same way, except that after choosing a sub-graph it is removed and replaced by a randomly generated one.

Using an angle of 90 degrees – a field of frameworks: evolving L-systems to satisfy load and constraints

These examples are based on a 3D L-system which initially just provides a generic branching machine based on the isospatial array (or dodecahedral lattice) borrowed from John Frazer. This was intended to provide as far as possible a neutral morphology for the phenotypes and, in particular, to avoid the tyranny of the orthogonal array, although such forms were quite possible as the isospatial is a superset of the normal cubic world, as evidenced by the early 'flytrap' experiments (see page 110) where the tendency for the basic embryology to grow banching clumps can be forced to adopt a planar morphology.

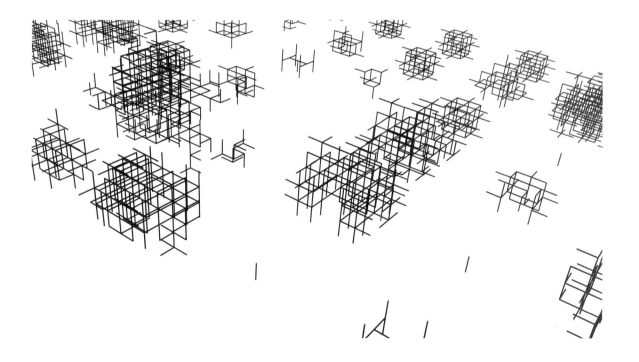

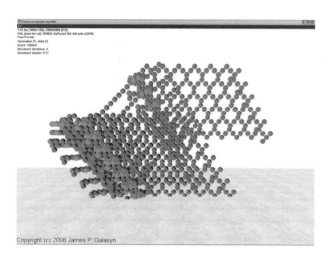

The flytrap experiment

Individuals are placed in an environment where a stream of particles are moving past the developing phenotype. The task is to evolve a strucure to trap the maximum particles using the minimum material, resulting in the L-system evolving into a flat sheet.

Evolution of the flytrap – below the history of seven generations from formless blob to sheet. The left example is of the fittest phenotype with fitness graph. The fitness function is:

number of hits x benefit of hit – number of balls x cost of balls

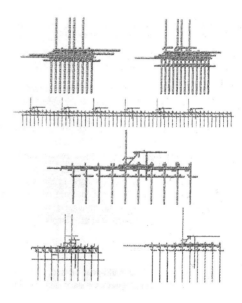

(*above*) One of Jim Galasyn's flytraps
(*right*) Family of evolved three-dimensional isospatial structures (Coates and Jackson, 1998)

Evolving the Body Plan

One of the examples of a 'good' Body Plan, as evidenced by zoological examples, is the adoption of both segmentation and <u>bilateral</u> symmetry. In the Genetic Algorithm example these developmental ideas must be explicitly coded in, but in the GP system it is possible to evolve them. In the illustration left (by Helen Jackson), the object evolved both segmentation and bilateral symmetry (unfortunately not visible in the illustrations as the vertical legs are splayed out in side view, not recorded here). It is interesting to note that the results are never 'perfect', but contain within themselves artefacts of their evolutionary history, like the appendix in our bodies as it were. The object in Helen's project was under evolutionary pressure to be stable under gravity as were Jim Galasyn's co-evolutionary towers, and in addition to conform to certain size and shape constraints, but the interesting outriggers on the top, once included in the genome, got stuck in there (maybe waiting for a chance to evolve into some other new constraint?).

In the following examples the functions are geometric manipulations of form, and the genotype is evaluated to produce 3D objects. In particular, the functions are AutoLISP functions that call AutoCAD operations by using both artificial selection and natural selection.

The way in which such trees of CAD functions are organised is based on embedding and recursion, which are the natural way in which LISP data structures and programs are created (in fact there is no conceptual difference between a list data structure and a program, one is the other), and there is a parallel with phrase structure grammars (which were developed by Chomsky, who was mentioned in Chapter 1) which define natural language in similar ways. Generating Automatically Defined Functions (ADFs) could be seen as a method of isolating useful sub-clauses in the evolving language.

Using Genetic Programming as a generative grammar of form

It is this close connection between the representation that leads us to talk of design grammars, in a more technical sense than <u>George Stiny</u>, with we hope the added bonus that a computational model allows automatic exploration of design spaces defined.

Grammars of the dom-ino house

We know what the initial grammar produces, when the simplest sentence produces the most basic design. GP allows the parallel exploration of the design worlds defined by the initial axioms and productions. Whether this is likely to be interesting depends entirely on the initial grammar. A badly chosen set of axioms and productions may lead to small design worlds. With a well-chosen grammar, leading to a large number of non-trivial design worlds, the likelihood of finding a suitable candidate as the solution to a properly posed problem increases.

GP allows the evolution of rule sets expressed as LISP functions, starting with a small defined set of primitives and CAD functions. The recognition part is, on the one hand, handled automatically by the EVAL function, and at the higher semantic level is of course provided globally on the entire phenotype by the user, who selects parents for breeding.

The standard eval function in lisp has a similar way of first 'recognising' a function and substituting the function with the evaluated result. Expressions such as (<u>union</u> (sub b1 b2) b3) have the effect of replacing the expression with its evaluation – an AutoCAD selection set of 3D solids.

Evolving a grammar (emergent typologies)

A grammar, as has already been discussed, is in this context a formal description of what semantic elements exist in a language, and the rules defined for how they can be defined (the syntax). The semantic elements (the words that carry the meaning) in this case are the primitive elements of the geometry (like nouns) and a repertoire of geometric operations like move, copy, etc. (like verbs). The syntax of this grammar is defined by the function tree syntax that GP uses.

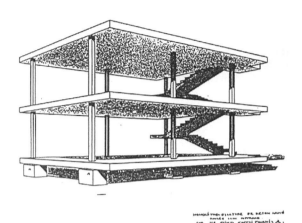

```
(dosubtract (box0)

  (dounion
    (dounion
      (copyback (box3) (box3))
      (copyrt (box1)(box1))
    )
    (dounion (box2) (box4))
  )
)
```

The code (above) when evaluated produces the very simplified object below. The function diagram illustrates the structure of the code

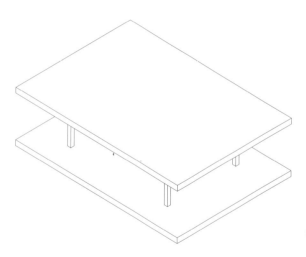

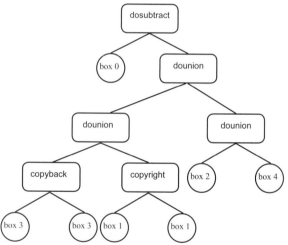

Genetic Programming syntax

The syntax of GP is based on the structure of a function tree. This is an (upside down) branching tree structure of functions and terminals, where the functions are the branches and the terminals are the leaves. The rule is that functions can have any number of branches, but terminals have none. In the case of this grammar, the functions are the verbs, and the terminals are the nouns. A tree of functions to make the initial dom-ino house looks like the code on the facing page.

Notice how the verb functions (drawn as rounded rectangles) are always connected to other verbs or nouns below them, but the nouns (drawn as circles) never have any. The interesting thing about such a tree is that it is a representation of a sentence in LISP, which being translated into English goes like this:

'Subtract from box 0 the result of Unioning the result of copying back box3 and box3 with the result of copying right the result of moving back everything copied right after copying back both box2 and box2 and box1 and box1.'

The important point about this syntax is that it is understood by the lisp interpreter so that we can write (EVAL(dounion (copyback . . . etc., etc. . . .))) in LISP and the computer will look up the appropriate functions to generate a simplified dom-ino house straight away with no messing!

Why the dom-ino house?

The dom-ino house has a special place in the history of architecture. It forms part of the early twentieth-century project founded by the rationalists to go back to the beginning of form, and to base all architectonics on sound engineering principles. Le Corbusier proposed that this canonical form provided a seed from which a large range of architectural objects could be elaborated. Luckily Le Corbusier was too much of a poet to be bound by his axiom, but his dom-ino idea became a powerful propaganda tool for lesser designers who used the basic concrete frame to spawn a million banalities. The GP dom-ino project is an attempt to explore the morphological implications of his idea, and perhaps to rescue the axiom from its later reductive adherents. By using the reconfiguration possibilities of the GP, it is possible to explore many more of the morphologies inherent in the basic pattern. It is also convenient that Le Corbusier's axiom was strictly orthogonal, as

this made the programming of the morphological generators much more straightforward and easier to understand than more complex initiators. Whatever the merits or otherwise of Le Corbusier's axiom, it is still interesting to observe the outcomes as an example of the possible extrapolations generated from any axiom.

Additive or subtractive? Embryologies of form

There are always two conceptually different ways of generating form using a 3D database of primitive blocks – the additive, where the base objects are combined in assemblies, and the subtractive, where the solid geometry is the emergent property of Boolean operations on overlapping solids. The former approach is that of the carpenter or bricklayer, the latter involves operations like moulding and casting, cutting and drilling out of large blocks (as in mechanical engineering).

In 1967 Peter Eisenman set out a sequence of morphological experiments (fin d'ou t haus) which (in a commentary by Geoffrey Broadbent, *A Plain Man's Guide to the Theory of Signs in Architecture* 1978)) were compared with Chomsky's transformational grammar of 1957 (*Syntactic Structures* (1957)). While fin d'ou t haus contained a number of elegant illustrations, it was only loosely algorithmic in the sense that the diagrams were drawn by hand and, at the time (and whether or not it was ever contemplated by Eisenman), it was not feasible to compute Boolean intersections in 3D solids. Boolean operations are computationally very expensive and were not available for the users of standard CAD software until the late 1990s (the earliest paper on Computational Solid Geometry is I. C. Braid's *Designing with Volumes* (1974)).

Following from this theoretical work on the combinatorial possibilities of Boolean operations in form (constructive solid geometry), the dom-ino GP was written as both a vocabulary of union/difference/subtract and the assembly operations of move and copy. This provides a powerful set of generators because the initial five blocks can produce a wide range of possible options given that every Boolean operation has four possible outcomes.

Emergent vocabularies of form

As explained earlier in the Genetic Algorithm artificial selection (dog breeding) example, the evolution of the morphology is based on the interaction between

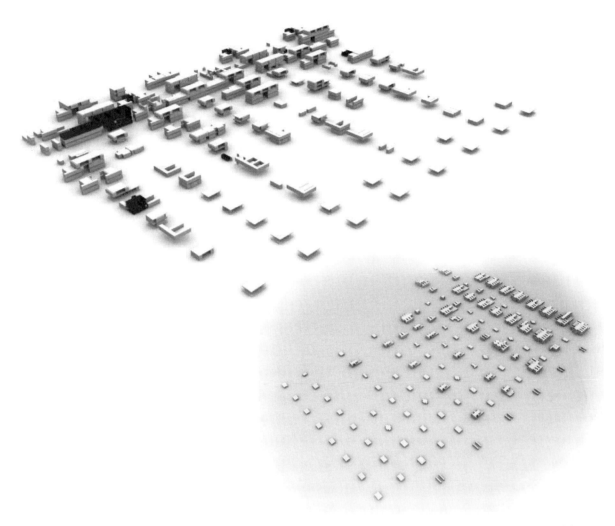

Histories of runs of the GP

the user and the program. In the case of the polyline program this is a simple shuffling of parameters, so that the best we can expect is that one particular combination will generate the morphology we need/would like. In the case of GP we are shuffling functions rather than parameters, in the hope that we will be able to break out of the restrictions imposed by simple Genetic Algorithms. During the run of one interaction with the GP system, the initial functions of the dom-ino house provide the seed for the evolution, the base set of functions. As the user selects promising individuals, those functions are combined with the crossover operation and, depending on the mutation rate, the mutation function inserts random new function trees from the pool of available functions and terminals. Meanwhile, randomly selected sub-trees are copied from the selected parents during the breeding process, and are stored in the pool. These are the automatically defined functions which are also available to the mutate function for insertion into new genomes.

Using ADFs has the effect of increasing the semantic depth of the genotype/phenotype by providing self-referencing sub-components which are slowly accumulated in successful (much chosen) phenotypes. As an example, the table on page 116 sets out the 15 ADFs generated during an interactive session of six generations. Looking at the table it is clear that these automatically extracted sub-trees get more complex as the user continues to select parents for breeding.

Another way of expressing this is to say that the diagram is drawn with the first big L shape enclosing the f9 and f2 shapes to represent the idea that, in the ADF, 15 function 2 is called first with 9 and 2 as

arguments. This is an example of recursive embedding, where f2 calls itself as one of its own arguments and is a nice example of how the outcome is not just the result of a kind of collage or random sticking together of base components. It is also interesting to note that the complexity of the phenotype (measured by the number of visible components and their geometrical relationships) is not accompanied by a huge increase in complexity of the genotype as represented by the ADF. In the GP algorithm, the sub-trees extracted as ADFs are restricted to be only of depth two or three, but while this certainly results in ADFs of similar size and restricted depth, the recursive recombination of ADFs allows the expansion of the function to become arbitrarily large – as in f15 on page 117.

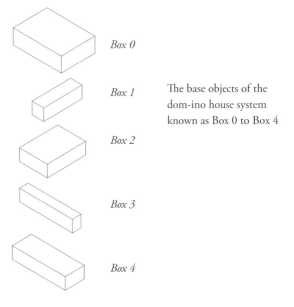

The base objects of the dom-ino house system known as Box 0 to Box 4

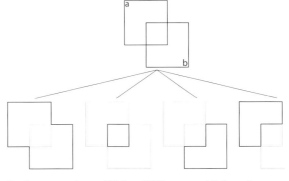

Boolean operations of Union, Difference and Subtractions B-A & A-B provide four different emergent geometries from the same starting configuration of solids

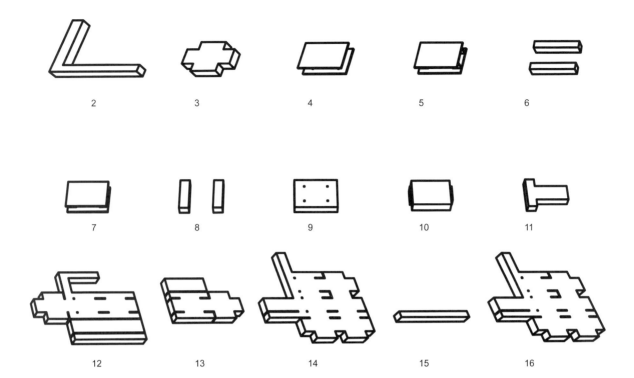

Table of emergent automatically defined functions (ADFs) generated by one run of the program. Each of these patterns represents a 3D object generated by a particular sub-tree selected automatically from 'fit' parents. ADF2 is very common in successful phenotypes, and various versions of the original 'dom-ino' show up (some with walls rather than columns). Note, ADFs 0, 1 and 17 are not shown.

Lemmas of form

Automatically defined functions in the dom-ino GP – a worked example

In this run we can see that by ADF function 15, quite a complex layout of walls, columns and partitions has been evolved out of the original dom-ino expression. On inspecting the text of the function it shows that it has embedded in itself a reference to function 2 (twice) and function 9. The tree diagrams show the structure of ADFs 2 9 and 15. The code for ADF F15 looks lke this:

```
(2 (9 P1 P2) (2 P3 P4 P5 P6) (COPYLT P7
   P8) (COPYFORWARD P9 P10)))))
```

So what this means is that we are doing a function 2 on function 9 and *itself* (see diagram at the bottom of the page). This provides a built-in reflexivity in the outcomes, allowing for basic patterns in the original grammar to be not only duplicated, but recursively embedded and elaborated at many different scales. The diagram sets out graphically what happens, but the text actually describes exactly how it happens, and the EVAL process will embody it as a 3D solid.

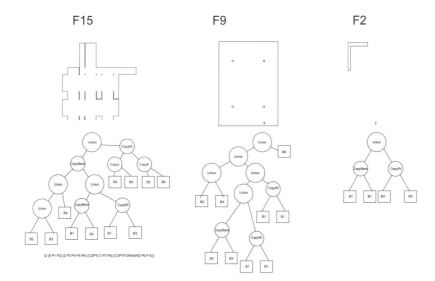

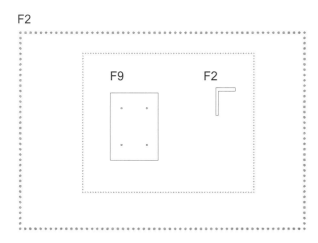

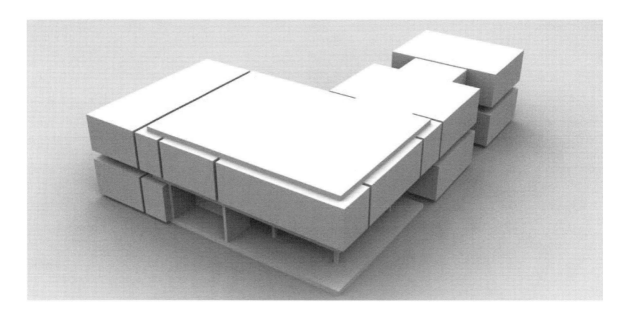

(DOSUBTRACT (COPYUP2 (4 (MOVEBACK (BOX4) (BOX3)) (1 (BOX4) (BOX2)) (DOUNION
(BOX1) (BOX4)) (COPYRT (BOX2) (BOX2))) (DOINTERSECT (BOX1) (BOX4))) (DOUNION
(DOUNION (COPYBACK (BOX3) (BOX3)) (COPYRT (BOX1) (BOX1))) (DOUNION (8 (BOX2)
(DOINTERSECT (BOX4) (BOX1)) (COPYFORWARD (BOX1) (BOX4)) (BOX4)) (DOUNION (BOX2)
(BOX4)))))

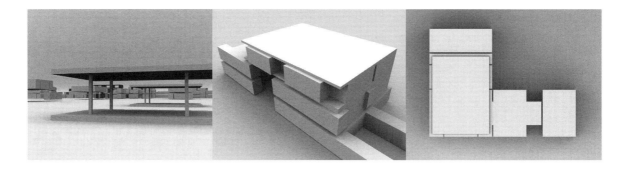

Emergent vocabularies of form

As explained earlier, the evolution of the morphology is based on the interaction between the user and the program. In the case of the evolving building program, this is a simple shuffling of parameters, so that the best we can expect is that one particular combination will generate the profile we need/would like. In the case of GP we are shuffling functions rather than parameters, in the hope that we will be able to break out of the restrictions imposed by simple Genetic Algorithms. During the run of one interaction with the GP system, the initial functions of the dom-ino house provide the seed for the evolution, the base set of functions. As the user selects promising individuals, those functions are combined with the crossover operation and, depending on the mutation rate, the mutation function inserts random new function trees from the pool of available functions and terminals. Meanwhile, randomly selected sub-trees are copied from the selected parents during the breeding process, and stored in the pool. These are the automatically defined functions which are also available to the mutate function for insertion into new genomes.

Using ADFs has the effect of increasing the semantic depth of the genotype/phenotype by providing self-referencing sub-components which are slowly accumulated in successful (much chosen) phenotypes. As an example, the table in the previous discussion sets out the 17 ADFs generated during an interactive session of six generations. Looking at the table it is clear that these automatically extracted sub-trees get more complex as the user continues to select parents for breeding. Another example of what Angeline called 'emergent intelligence', but which in this context can be called an emergent spatial organisation and shows the end product after six generations and its genotype. In this case it has used ADFs 0, 1, 4 and 8. Thus the image on the left represents a design represented by the text below it.

This shows that the underlying proportion and operations of the grammar carry across to partition space into appropriately grammatical configurations, and that 'well-formed' configurations proliferate with a base set of phrases (ADFs) derived from the atomic verbs.

It is also interesting to note that similar phrases, such as ADF 4 and ADF7, occur in many runs but *do not* give rise to very similar end product phenotypes.

It is also noticeable that the original dom-ino house genotype has been turned into an ADF (for instance 4 and 5). In such ways we can see that the GP system has evolved a higher order vocabulary from the primitives and that these design phrases could form the basis of new grammars derived from the canonical examples. It is a kind of architectural analysis of Le Corbusier's statement into not the smallest particles, but those fragments capable of carrying architectural meaning.

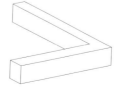
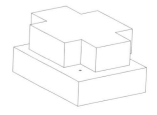

ADFs 0, 1, 4 and 8

Generally this chapter has been concerned with looking at how one might define a 'language of architecture' as a programming language. The disadvantage of this project is that programming languages are totally explicit and mechanical devices, and most designers would obviously baulk at codifying their entire architectural approach in such a formal way. The advantage, however, is that even very simple languages, once defined, can allow us to experiment and generate form because the computer, once we are talking its language, will tirelessly produce sentences in the language. The outcomes from the dom-ino GP sessions show that, by using a recombinable grammar, we can evolve higher order words and clauses in these artificial languages that may point to richer and more complex outcomes which are nevertheless legal (syntactically correct), and where we can even talk about emergent semantics such as the L shape and other emergent phrases.

This chapter has been following the implications of the initial assertion that the text of code is the only text that can read and write itself. Through the development of production systems to a generative grammar of form, we have seen ways of explicitly coding for shape ideas, and even developing a metalanguage to evolve new grammars of form.

Starting with the initial *axiom* of a production system, it has led on to formal descriptions of shape operations that led to lemmas of form (that is, a subsidiary proposition that can be used as the basis for a proof). In that sense the illustration opposite is the proof, and therefore the named functions can be seen as emergent subsidiary propositions leading to that proof – or design.

Google Earth view of part of Timbuktu Mali

chapter five

Text of the vernacular

The study of 'unplanned' settlements is traditionally closely allied to the view from 30,000 feet, the elicitation of global forces like geography, topography, economics, society, culture and so on. It is possible to seriously annoy senior academics by insisting that the form of unplanned settlements is not best described by a-spatial measures, or at least that the shape and detailed pattern of the settlement can be explained in spatial terms. Similarly, where they can bring themselves to look, the architectural observers usually deal with the physical reality of the barrio/favela/etc. in strictly picturesque terms.

The idea that the morphology of unofficial agglomerations of buildings can be studied using algorithmic simulations is not original, and can be dated back at least 40 years (the author himself has had a hand in several examples), but in order to be respectable such simulations are invariably subjected to a global analysis and reading of the outcomes. Examples can be found in Hillier's axial analysis and other network analysis tools; see Space Syntax.

This could be said to be the 'weak' version of the algorithmic representation of emergent morphology, placing the status of the analysis above that of the generative script itself. However, in accordance with the intention of the book, the 'strong' version is presented, where the algorithm of the generating script is given the status of an explanation in itself. The three levels of observation are developed, from the global to the various degrees of local, and it is pointed out that the real observer is the person on the ground who lives in the texture and succession of spaces and perspectives to be found in such morphologies. The suggestion is that the bottom-up algorithms presented in this section map well onto the actual (supposed) processes of agglomeration that can be retrieved from various vernaculars around the world, where varieties of local actors make many kinds of local decisions.

This approach can be seen as a kind of rehabilitation of the picturesque and the redefinition of the author; that very English preoccupation which was shared by many unlikely visionaries including the Archigram group and the whole informal architecture movement of Cedric Price and others in the mid-twentieth century.

This series illustrates the way that generative models can be seen as 'proof of concept' models for the use of simulation to explore descriptions of space. It is problematic for 'traditional' epistemologies to rely on simulations as a way of describing something, but in the case of complex urban structures of space there is some reason to attempt it. These experiments were developed from the fundamental principles set out in von Foerster and Zopf's semial work *Principles of Self-organisation* (1962).

First, the conventional description is highly complex and tendentious, since the subject of study has developed say over the previous 2,000 years, and (as with all informal development) there are very few records of what and why various configurations occur. In this case it seems worthwhile to try to tackle the problem by hypothesising very simple rules, whose output generates complexity by means of feedback loops implied by the process, as illustrated by the Alpha Syntax model overleaf.

Non-specific structure

To be any use as a description it is vital not to over specify the problem, otherwise the results will be tautologous – already containing the instructions required to produce the outcome, rather than letting the outcome emerge from the interaction of simpler, more general rules. Gordon Pask set out the principle of 'epistemic autonomy' for the simulation, in order to generate 'structural autonomy'.

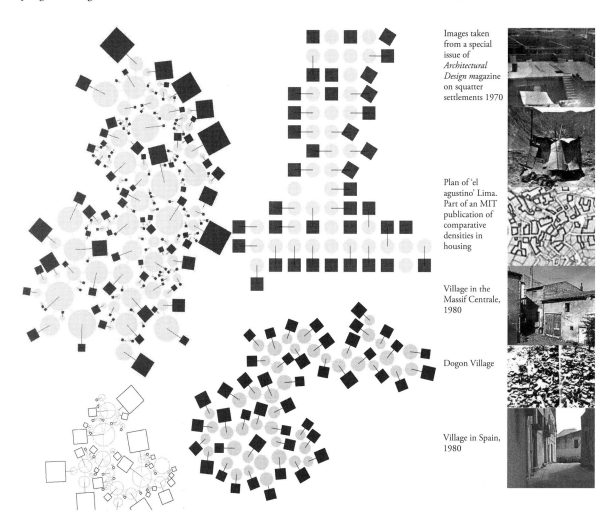

Images taken
from a special
issue of
*Architectural
Design* magazine
on squatter
settlements 1970

Plan of 'el
agustino' Lima.
Part of an MIT
publication of
comparative
densities in
housing

Village in the
Massif Centrale,
1980

Dogon Village

Village in Spain,
1980

Some images from the Alpha Syntax model with varying parameters for size and geometry

Status of the observer

As we saw in earlier chapters, in a simulation the observer needs to be a well-defined part of the system. In NetLogo (used to make some of the explanatory diagrams of emergent space) there is a formal definition of the observer, who is a software agent with strictly limited global operations, as opposed to the individuals in the cellular array of patches or collection of agents. It is also important to remember the role of the human author/experimenter, who interacts by taking samples and judging outcomes subjectively. In the 1970s experiments (described in case studies 1 and 2 overleaf), the outcomes were snapped from the screen using a 16 mm camera with fast colour film, as the simulations were

running. As various features were observed and logged, so it became easier to spot them in later runs.

The agglomerative models are 'ill defined' in Pask's and Ashby's definition, and the outcomes (observables) are a set of 'distinctions' that can be made between the spatial organisation that emerges from these simulations and the top-down spatial systems traditionally held up as observables (streets, squares, etc.). The cul-de-sac that emerges in the `damascene model' (case study 1) is one of these observables not directly built into the rules for the model, which makes it possible to say that the algorithm captures some fundamental process rather than mimicking the 'look' of the spatial structure observed.

Randomness and its status in the model

In all the following models the main driver of the complexity of the output is the use of random numbers in the code. These are generated by a variety of algorithms, and being computer programs, they are all completely deterministic, with any particular random series set by an arbitrary 'seed' number. Such routines are conventionally provided for statisticians and provide a bias-free noise against which the algorithm must play. There are a number of ways of checking that the number stream is bias free, and provided that this is the case then any result can be interpreted as one of a number of 'equally likely' outcomes.

Chaos theory tells us that what are seemingly random events can often (or always for hardened observers) be explained as the complex outcome of purely deterministic processes. Manfred Schroeder (*Fractals, Chaos, Power Laws*, 1991) demonstrates a range of very simple algorithms (calculation of PI, Fibonacci series, and many others taken from number theory), all of which yield 'unpredictable' results. There are a number of algorithms which can be used to generate random numbers as a by-product of their operation, one good example is the Swarm (discussed in Chapter 3), where the many calculations of the swarming agents – each of which is chasing the tail of another and so on reflexively for ever – can be used as a bias-free driver for complex behaviour without needing any extra random number algorithms.

So random numbers can be generated by many deterministic algorithms, and the model builder would do well to select one such which can be shown to be appropriate to the system being modelled. In the case of the models described here, this is not the case and that must be seen as a failing.

Obviously it is not possible to replace the random choices of placement by historical data, neither is it practicable to invoke the actual complexity of the 'real world', but for now they must stand or fall on their status as very simple algorithms embedded in a noisy environment, where the noise represents the unknown and unknowable agglomerative behaviours of actual builders over long times.

Case study 1

To see if there is a simple way of modelling spatial structures found in the common 'courtyard type housing'. These cities have developed in the Mediterranean and Middle East over the last 5,000 years, of which Damascus is the canonical example – although many examples can be found in ancient cities elsewhere.

Assumptions:
- That these urban systems developed by slow agglomeration of individual building decisions.
- That at any time, all the buildings have to be accessible to each other and the main parts of the town.
- That there are some predefined or agreed global structures for access (main street).

The model starts as an undifferentiated plane, but with some areas marked out as 'streets'. This is represented by a grid of squares (a 2D array of integers which can be labelled, e.g. 'empty', 'house' or 'main street'). During the run of the program, 'houses' are fired randomly at this surface, and checks are made:

1. that the putative house doesn't cover road cells;
2. that it has at least one open side accessible to the road – this is checked by testing all possible routes from all neighbouring empty cells to see if an unbroken chain of cells exists to a road cell; and
3. if this is the case, then draw the house, otherwise carry on with the next random location.

This process of establishing whether or not a possible location is legal is the basis of the algorithm described as the Damascene model below. While the English description above is clear, the inclusion of the search of 'all possible routes' seems a little daunting, given the open-ended nature of the problem and complexity of these possible routes. The solution is to generalise the problem into doing something quite simple over and over again (recursively).

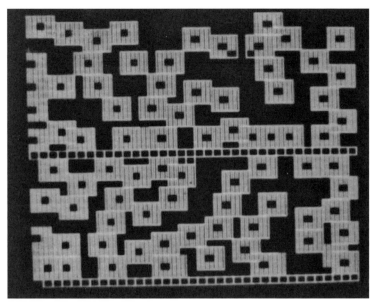

Output from the model displayed on a tektronix 4010 graphic display, generated in BASIC on a Data General Nova <u>minicomputer</u> around about 1977

Case study 1

To see whether there is a simple way of modelling spatial structures found in pre-Islamic cities like the one in the photograph.

The idea of accessibility in these early experiments was crudely represented by a row of 'street' cells. It was because everyone was trying to get to just that one street that the culs-de-sac formed the way they did. It is prohibitively time consuming to test literally whether you can get from anywhere to anywhere else, so you just see whether everyone can get to one (and the same) place. To check that a house can reach a bit of main street, use the *floodfill* algorithm. This works by starting out from the house and stepping from cell to cell where they are empty, until either you reach a street cell or you get stuck

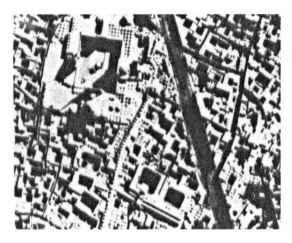

Aerial view of Damascus taken from Building Design *magazine in 1967*

The floodfill algorithm

There are two ways of looking at the floodfill algorithm, the 'ink blot' model and the 'infection' model. In 1977 the use of procedural programming and linear processing led to the ink blot version (sketched out in the diagram below). Starting from each of the possible surrounding cells, the pattern spreads out like a stain (numbered boxes), only covering the unoccupied cells, until it reaches a street cell (boxes labelled R). A commercial example of the floodfill algorithm is the bucket tool in Photoshop.

The INKBLOT or LEAK method

A location affects its neighbours, and this can be written as a recursive procedure something like this:

```
To flood (x, y)
if patch(x, y) is unoccupied
  then
    set patch 'occupied'
    flood (x+1, y)
    flood (x-1, y)
    flood (x, y+1)
    flood (x, y-1)
    else
    if patch(x,y) is road
    then exit success
exit failure
end
```

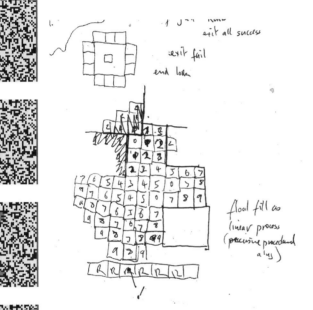

The INFECT method

However, using NetLogo, which acts as a parallel process on each cell, the infection model is more appropriate. Each cell asks its neighbours if they are flooded and, if so, sets itself to be flooded:

```
ask all cells simultaneously:
to flood
  get count of neighbours who are flooded
  if this patch is unoccupied
  then[if there are any flooded patches
  [setpatch to flooded ]]
end
```

NetLogo movie illustrating the progress of a floodfill starting on the left middle side and stopping at the line on the right

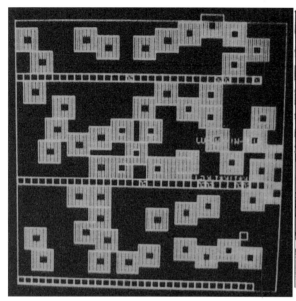

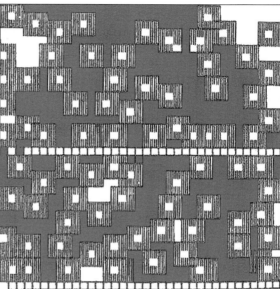

Model at an early stage of agglomeration

Model at an later stage of agglomeration

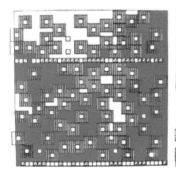

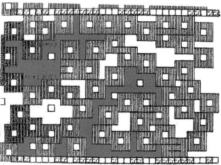

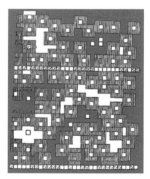

Observed outcomes of the Damascene model

In the diagrams on the left, the street spaces are the white squares, and the houses the grey shaded squares, which are 3 x 3 arrays of cells. The grey areas represent the emergent shape of the accessible space. These form culs-de-sac growing from the main streets, whose shape is determined by the accidental history of the agglomeration. Long irregular spaces (filled in grey) connect the houses to the streets, and smaller more compact spaces (white) are left behind, which are disconnected from the accessible passage areas.

This global morphology is not directly determined by the algorithm, in fact of course the rules as they operate produce a succession of overall shapes for the connecting spaces, starting with a broad plain with a few bumps of houses, then going on to long connecting spaces, and, finally, as the density builds up, the long connecting spaces are broken by the last houses which divide the two-way passage into two one-way passages. The cul-de-sac is, as it were, the 'attractor' state, or the logical conclusion of this packing-in process.

So the cul-de-sac can be seen as one of the laws of form, it emerges without any special rules apart from the requirement of accessibility and highest density. When the Damascene-type cities are visited, however, it is often observed that the culs-de-sac and courts are often occupied by a single trade or guild, and this has been used to develop a social theory of courts, that they occur because people want to live and work together in social/guild groupings.

This model, however, shows that the courts will happen anyway, and that perhaps the social organisation is an adventitious occupation of a 'natural' morphogenetic process.

Occam's Razor/the new epistemology

At the very least it offers a simple description for the observed morphology rather than the complex anthropological one, relying on laws and customs of societies gone by. There are only two constraints:

1. No point in building a house if you cannot get to it.
2. Go on increasing density until you cannot fit any more in.

Of course there could be further refinements including allowing demolition, and more subtle modelling of individual houses with subdivision and amalgamation altering the accessibility constraint. Some of these refinements are considered in the later alpha syntax models. The model can be criticised for its assumptions, primarily the assumption of given 'streets', to which the emerging morphology must be connected, and secondly the assumption that the ground is universally walkable on, right from the beginning of the simulation.

In desert climates it may be possible to assume that the universal plane is immediately available for use (aerial photographs of the outskirts of desert settlements in the Middle East show individual courtyard houses surrounded by cars and using the desert to drive on), but for a more general model, suitable for rainy muddy situations, the roads themselves should also be seen as 'figure' rather than 'ground'. In fact, generalising from the specific urban agglomeration model to a more general served/ service idea allows the roads to be seen as growing on their own account as service systems with the houses as agglomerative elements clustering at the tips of roads.

Mutually amplifying feedback loops

The emergence of global patterns of culs-de-sac, and in particular the particular sorts of morphology observed, are an example of 'deviation amplifying feedback' and 'mutual causality' introduced by Magoroh Maruyama in 1963. This is important because it underlies all of the experiments in this section, where the global outcome (the observed morphology) is the result of the history of the process starting from some seed condition, where at each moment decisions have to be made about the placing of some element as a consequence of decisions so far, which will influence the placing of later elements forever after, which will, in turn, affect later placements and so on. Thus the initial irregularity is amplified and the interacting parts of the system affect each other, thus mutual causality. This mechanism can be translated into human activity in building by observing that:

1. it is usually easier to add to an existing agglomeration than demolish and rebuild;
2. it is cheaper to add to an existing building rather than build a stand alone version; and
3. demolition of large areas of an existing agglomeration cannot happen unless there is some advanced kind of social organisation which overrides individual occupant's wishes.

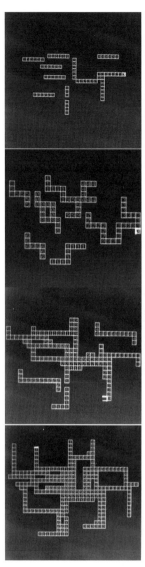

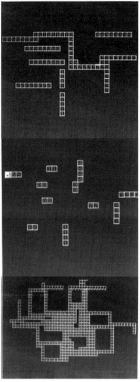

Pond slime model programmed in
Fortran on ICL1906A, paper tape
output, read into the DG Nova mini
and visualised using a small basic
program (about 1973)

Maruyama's description of the algorithm

The algorithm, as described in English. This is a classic
example and can be found in a few places on the web.

Let us imagine, for the sake of simplicity, a two-
dimensional organism. Let us further imagine that its
cells are squares of an equal size. Let us say that the
organism consists of four types of cells: green, red,
yellow, and blue (refer to image opposite).

Each type of cell reproduces cells of the same type to
build a tissue. A tissue has at least two cells. The tissues
grow in a two-dimensional array of squares. Let us give
a set of rules for the growth of tissues:

1. No cells die, a cell is always there.
2. Both ends of a tissue grow whenever possible,
    by reproducing one cell per unit time in a vacant
    contiguous square. If there is no vacant contiguous
    square at either end, that end stops growing.
    If there are more than one vacant contiguous
    squares at either end, the direction of the growth is
    governed by the preferential order given by Rules
    3, 4 and 5.
3. If, along the straight line defined by the end
    cell and the penultimate cell (next to the end
    cell), there are less than or equal to three cells of
    the same type (but may be of different tissues)
    consecutively, the preferred direction is along
    the same straight line. If that direction is blocked,
    follow Rule 5.
4. If, along the straight line defined by the end cell
    and the penultimate cell, there are more than or
    equal to four cells of the same type (but may be
    of different tissues) consecutively, the preferred
    direction of the growth is a left turn. If a left turn is
    impossible, make a right turn.
5. If, when a straight growth is preferred, the straight
    growth is impossible because the square ahead is
    already occupied, do the following: If the square
    to which the straight growth would take place is
    filled with a cell of the same type as the growing
    tissue, make a left turn. If the square ahead is filled
    with a cell whose type is different from that of the
    growing tissue, make a right turn.
6. The growth of the four types of tissue is, time-
    wise, out of phase with each other: green first, red
    second, yellow third, and blue last within a cycle of
    one unit time.

Case study 2

In order to develop the notion of mutually amplifying feedback, the next example sets out to explore the idea of the service/served idea above. The question is: 'Is there a way of modelling the relationship between streets and buildings in a way that makes both depend on the other?' A canonical model of linear self-organisation which might prove useful was Maruyama's pond slime model. In his paper he did not present any code and all the examples were worked out by hand, so this is a nice opportunity to develop a solution using a text based on his flow diagram from 1969.

The two state model – Maruyama's pond slime
The example Maruyama uses to demonstrate mutual causality is the pond slime algorithm. Here individual seeds of pond slime are modelled as simple growing cells consisting of two opposite growing ends. They are of several types, and where there is only one the initial seed will grow into a curled ball of material. This is because the rule is as follows:

1. Grow new material at opposite ends as long as there is not anything in the way.
2. When four new cells have grown, turn right.
3. If you bump into yourself, turn right also.
4. If you bump into somebody else, turn left.

This small difference between me and somebody else results in a complex intertwining of strands of pond slime, leading to the matted choking green mess that is the commonest outcome of this organism.

So starting with one cell, it first elongates then curls round on itself (this is what can be observed where very few initial cells are present in the pond). However, when a growing cell tip encounters a different bit of pond slime from itself, then a new rule is invoked.

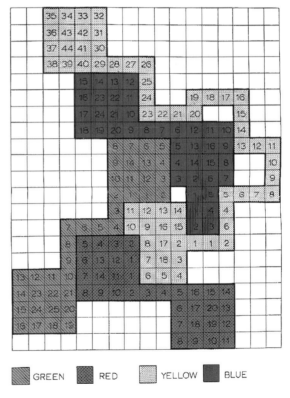

Converting this into a program to be written using NetLogo

First check if this is going to be possible. Looks like it is going to be easy, these first three specifications are right out of the box in NetLogo 2D. Basically this describes a series of patches.

The first decision to make is: should we use just patches of perhaps, as it says here, leave the patches as the underlying grid and see the organism as turtles? As always we have to ask which is more natural and appropriate to the algorithm. Since it talks of 'growing' and reproducing, it seems that it should be turtles, as the patches are always there from the start and do not have a concept of growing.

So, it looks like we start with one turtle and try to define 'both ends', since looking ahead to Rules 3, 4 and 5 we see that there is a concept of directionality and turning. This is *great*! Turtles have headings, they can go forward, turn left and right, and so on, so it looks like this is going to be easy.

We start looking at the setup procedure by scattering some turtles, giving a random heading between up, left, right, down (here we give the turtles different colours, just so we can see them).

```
ask turtles
  [
  set heading random 4 * 90
  set color who + 20
  hatch 1[set heading heading + 180]
  ]
```

The hatch command asks every turtle to hatch a child, in every respect identical to its parent, but with the heading reversed, so if mum was heading north, hatchling is facing south, etc.

Looking at Rule 3 we see that there is an idea of the 'length' that the turtles have moved, and also one of 'is me is not me'. The identity of 'me or not 'can be easily handled by making sure the colour of each turtle and its child are a specific colour based on the parent's unique ID (called the who). As well as this, how will we know how long the organism is?

This is a very good example of altering the question to make it easier to code. You might think we should somehow measure the cells by looking over our shoulder, but the trick here is to get a turtle to know how many steps it has taken. Set this to 1 at the first step, and add 1 to each time we move. Then if you need to know whether it is time to fire Rule 4, check your personal 'steps' counter.

Another thing that is not immediately obvious is, if we are using the colour of a turtle to indicate the type (same type/different type; as in the flow chart on the previous page), how do we check this? The decision I took was that, since we are colouring in the grid anyway, we can look at that to check who it is. So we must make the turtles colour in the patches that they grow over/walk on.

Then when this is all done we get everyone to take a step:

```
ask turtles
  [
  set pcolor color fd 1 set pcolor color
  set steps 1
  ]
```

Here we colour in the patch we are standing on and move one ahead, and also increment our stepcounter. After this we are ready to write the main loop, obeying the Rules 2 to 5, but hold on! What is this in Rule 6 about timewise out of step? Remember this algorithm is intended to be a formal description of the emergence of complexity with respect to, for instance, colonies of very simple organisms. Surely a real colony just goes ahead simultaneously, not in a turn-taking manner? We shall choose to ignore this rule for now as we can experiment with different scheduling schemes later if we like.

Coding the rules

The first rule to deal with is:

2. Both ends of a tissue grow whenever possible, by reproducing one cell per unit time in a vacant contiguous square.

The idea of growing wherever possible is a kind of meta rule, which applies to the whole algorithm.

NetLogo has a very useful turtle command 'patch-ahead', which precisely models the idea of 'vacant contiguous square':

```
ifelse pcolor-of (patch-ahead 1) = white
```

This asks a turtle to look one patch ahead to see whether the patch that it is just about to step on is free.

4. If, along the straight line defined by the end cell and the penultimate cell, there are more than or equal to four cells of the same type (but may be of different tissues) consecutively, the preferred direction of the growth is a left turn. If a left turn is impossible, make a right turn.

The 'straight line defined by the end cell and the penultimate cell' is the turtle's current heading, the idea of the 'more than or equal to four cells' is handled by the mod function where branchlength = 4:

```
if (steps mod branchlength) = 0 [left 90]
```

The choice of turn is done by:

```
[ifelse pcolor-of (patch-ahead 1) = color
   [left 90]  ;left if it is me
   [right 90] ;right if it is somebody else
]
```

The 'am I blocked by myself' rule is expressed, as is the patch-ahead the same colour as me (here we just say 'color' because this is the turtle talking in American).

Finally Rule 2 also states: 'If there is no vacant contiguous square at either end, that end stops growing':

```
[
  ;now we have turned or not one final
     check for room to grow
  ifelse pcolor-of (patch-ahead 1) = white
    [fd 1 set pcolor color set steps steps
        + 1]
    [die]
]
```

NetLogo outcome of pond slime model

Notice that the order of the rules is different from the
list from Maruyama. The are many different ways we
can schedule the process (including the turn-taking
four-colour turtles used in the Fortran experiments
on page 130). The code below is just a simple stab at
getting this thing to work in a Parallel kind of way. It
contains two ASKs: one to sort out which way to turn,
and one to check it is ok to go. Since a turtle's heading is
entirely relative (turtle drawing as in the examples of the
L-systems and other projects earlier), this code works
for either end of the pond slime, and for any particular
orientation. A more free-form (realistic) pond slime
model would be to use only turtles (the reader is invited
to attempt this!):

```
ask turtles
   [

   ;one off check to see if it is time to turn
   if (steps mod branchlength) = 0 [left 90]

   ;room to grow checks
   if pcolor-of (patch-ahead 1) != white ;seem to be stuck

      [ifelse pcolor-of (patch-ahead 1) = color
        [left 90]  ;left if it is me
        [right 90] ;right if it is somebody else
      ]
   ]

;all turtles have done the turns now time to move
ask turtles
   [

   ;now we have turned or not one final check for room to grow
      ifelse pcolor-of (patch-ahead 1) = white
      [fd 1 set pcolor color set steps steps + 1]
      [die]

   ]
if count turtles = 0 [stop]

end
```

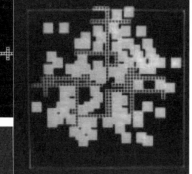

The global form of the resulting agglomeration is mostly controlled by the initial positions of the seeds for the street system, and the probabilities of scattering for the houses. The illustrations show single and four seed systems, plus one single seed which has had to adopt a linear form due to early blockage of the horizontal component.

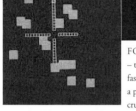

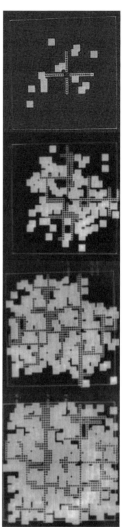

FORTRAN experiments from 1973 using the same equipment as the Maruyama example – the ICL 1906 A only had 16K words of memory, but was capable of processing lots of data fast. Visualisation was done on the Nova/Textronix 1410 terminal, data being loaded from a paper tape punched out by the mainframe. Thus the job was split between the number cruncher using Fortran and the mini running a small program in BASIC, but with a graphics display. To move data from one machine to the other, one walked with the punched cards one way, and the paper tape the other.

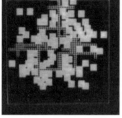

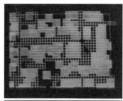

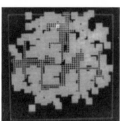

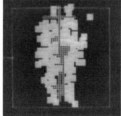

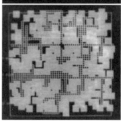

Clustering buildings and roads

Maruyama's model was presented as an example of 'deviation amplifying feedback' and is, according to the author, an example of 'second order cybernetics'. In 1963 this meant that this was a model of emergent complexity rather than the (then) traditional control system model of Ashby and Ross.

As the growing pattern of cells (hollow squares) occurs, the pond slime mechanism falls into two behaviours:

1. simple coiled loops (where the cell intersects itself); and
2. long irregular threads (where the cell intersects another pond slime).

The pond slime algorithm forms the basis of the street growing rules. The original flow diagram and rules are shown on page 131. This behaviour is adapted in the street version so that cells always branch after n growth units, and, if no houses are met, will generate a simple grid (top left image). However, if a house is met, then the growing network will take avoiding action.

Meanwhile the agglomerative sprinkle system works by scattering 'houses' near the growing tips of the street system. Various different morphologies can be created by varying the density of scattering, and by seeding the street growing system at several points, or just one. Houses are not allowed to overlap existing street cells, but can overlap existing houses.

Thus the 'deviation amplifying feedback', which Maruyama demonstrated between two different individuals (of the same species), is modified here to be between two different species, road stuff and house stuff – mutually feeding back to amplify any small irregularities in the pattern into larger clusters and lumps.

Observed outcomes

By varying the clustering rate and the branching rules, a wide range of courtyard clusters and streets could be seen, with 'rational' relationships between service and served components, such that the 'house stuff' was usually well served and accessible. The configurations were also of a wide variety, from mostly linear to very clustered. This was achieved by varying the clustering parameters – the likelihood that a growing road tip would attract a house, and the likelihood that a house would attract another house. There was also a road growth speed factor which determined how much road was developed per time cycle.

Thus the growing clusters had the effect of stopping the roads from growing, and so from attracting more houses, but the growing roads encouraged more houses, so it becomes a battle between roads and houses as to who wins the race. In this sense, 'designing' with this system was a matter of adjusting these parameters, observing the outcome, then running again.

Since the process was run on two different machines half a mile apart, with a certain amount of card feeding and paper tape carrying (not to mention sitting in front of the Nova with a bag over one's head and a camera with ultra fast colour film), the design cycle was quite tortuous.

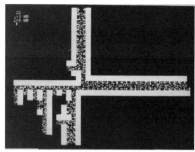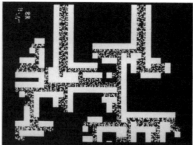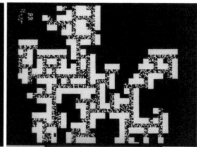

Screen shots of the original orthogonal A-syntax model, run
on UMIST's DEC 10 from Liverpool Polytechnic via a land
line. This time the graphics were generated by the mainframe.
We even had a thermal printer for screen shots off the
Tektronix 4010. (Funded by SRC seed grant in 1980.)

(*left*) High clustering
(*middle*) Medium clustering
(*right*) Low clustering

Altering the clustering parameters allowed the system to
model a range of syntaxes including 4 and 5

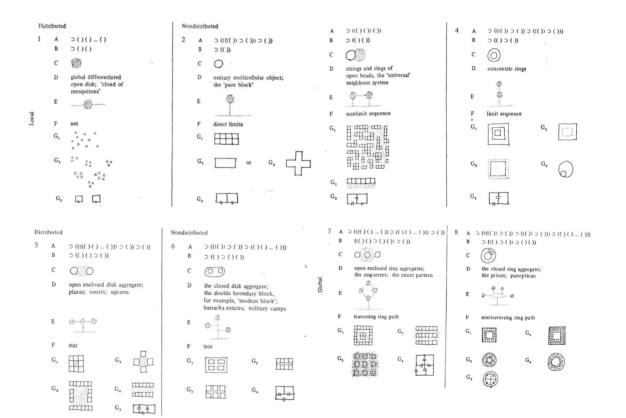

The original set of eight syntaxes. The one chosen to
experiment with was no. 3, the universal neighbour system

The Alpha Syntax model

A further refinement of the two state mode is based on Bill Hillier's original idea of a three state automaton which attempts to capture the essence of 'unplanned' organic village growth in Europe.

Closed – open space relation (X > Y)

Open – open space (Y > Y) relation

There are three types of cell, closed, open and 'nothing', referred to by Hillier in the original article (Hillier, 1976) as the carrier space. As with the previous model, there are two types of space – closed private 'inside' space (labelled 'X') and open public 'outside' space (labelled 'Y'). However, in this model the relationship between the two is more explicitly stated, with both types being coupled together such that each bit of private space is related to a bit of public space. Added to this is the crucial next rule in that each bit of public space is connected to another bit of public space. This was controlled by a special 'grid growing' pond slime algorithm in the previous model, but in this model there is no special rule about open space, other than it should be contiguous.

In the original paper there were any number of syntaxes, apart from the x > y relation there were xx > yx > yy and so on in increasing rigidity, but these latter ones did not give rise to any interesting varieties of morphology, being overconstrained.

The result of running the system is the gradual development of a network of open space elements, with 'houses' attached . The original version (illustrated in *The Social Logic of Space* (1984)) was cellular, with no extra rules, the illustrations (left) are examples of generating the standard cellular orthogonal model, but with added clustering parameters and the possibility of selecting their syntaxes. Hillier's approach is an elegant inversion of the original model, because the primary focus is on the space generated, whereas in the earlier models described (the Damascene model) the space is something left over after you had managed to locate the form.

Cellular Automata

The Hillier model also brings the mechanism of spatial agglomeration much closer to the standard Cellular Automaton (CA) than the earlier work. They can be seen as a method for describing spatial configurations and patterns of form as the emergent outcome of a discrete spatial and temporal simulation. A CA is always a parallel system, where all cells in the system decide whether to change state or not simultaneously, as opposed to the original Alpha Syntax where things happen one at a time. Whereas the earlier simulations described above were each unique and had different sub-systems programmed into them (such as street growing or house agglomeration), the CA is a general system which can be redefined to perform a number of different computations (including the agglomerative systems). Essentially a CA is:

- a surface divided into lots of identical cells in 1, 2, 3 or however many dimensions (examples here are 2D);
- for each cell, a series of possible states it can be in (usually represented as colours);
- for each cell, a set of rules about when to change state based on the number of neighbours; and
- for each cell, a defined neighbourhood (in 2D this is either 4 or 8 – see the Sana experiments).

This general-purpose overall-architecture of the CA makes it a very flexible system, which can be altered either by changing the number of states, the neighbourhood or the rules. One of the problems in designing a CA is that you cannot work backward from the configuration you want, to the rules, but you must try to experiment with different rules, run them and then inspect the outcome. This is characteristic of emergent computing, and is the downside of the great simplicity of the algorithm.

Running the parallel Alpha Syntax generator with the closed proportion of cells = 20% (*top*) gives a very large undifferentiated spatial configuration. With this value at 30% (*middle*) the system gets blocked by closed cells and develops a multi-branching system of open space with large enclosed inaccessible carrier space. Raising the proportion of closed cells to 40% results in closed off branches and small systems (*bottom*)

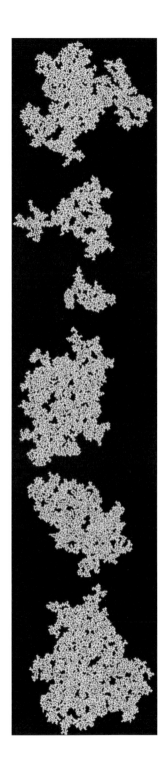

The Alpha Syntax village generator

In the same way that there are two ways of looking at the floodfill algorithm, the procedural/recursive and the parallel (using NetLogo), the Alpha Syntax algorithm can be expressed two ways:

1. Procedural/recursive

```
To grow (x, y)
  try one of
    neighbours of this patch at x, y
    to see if they can be a new openpatch
  if ok then
  try one of
    neighbours of this new openpatch
    to see if they can be a closed patch

    if ok then
  grow (newOpenpatch)
end
```

2. Parallel

```
to grow

if this patch = carrierspace then
  if it has openspace in its neighbourhood
      then
    on the toss of a coin
    turn openspace or closedspace
end
```

The parallel version is simpler, but because all the patches are evaluating simultaneously it is not possible to 'take turns' on setting open and then closed spaces, and it has to be done by chance. Because the original algorithm insists on each new closed cell having its own open cell (look to place open cell and then only if that is possible, place closed), whereas the parallel one cannot control this directly, the ratio of closed to open cells has to be lower than 50%, otherwise the system chokes itself off with the open space cells getting surrounded by closed ones. By experiment it can be found that a proportion of just below 40% is the maximum probability for closed cells still allowing growth.

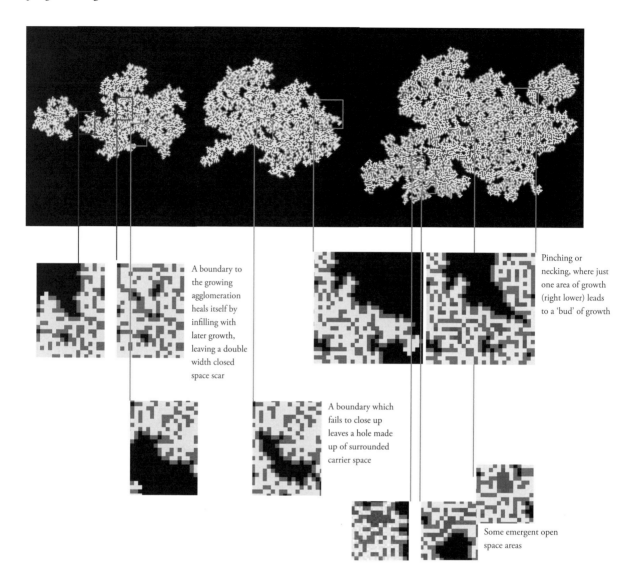

A boundary to the growing agglomeration heals itself by infilling with later growth, leaving a double width closed space scar

Pinching or necking, where just one area of growth (right lower) leads to a 'bud' of growth

A boundary which fails to close up leaves a hole made up of surrounded carrier space

Some emergent open space areas

Observations of the Alpha Syntax model

One of the ideas behind the original model was to explore the detailed morphology of unplanned (emergent) spatial organisation. As these early models were based on the grid, it was not possible to make very good observations at the local level (see the next section for the off the grid results). It was observed that running the model for a long time just resulted in large homogeneous systems of space which were everywhere much the same shape and size, i.e. the system failed to develop an overall global structure as can be observed happening in real village and town growth.

However, it is possible to make second-order observations on the emergent spatial configuration, as shown on this page where, after the simple Alpha Syntax has done its work, it is possible to assign different labels to specific spatial qualities:

1. If a patch of open space is completely surrounded by road space patches, then it becomes a Y-Y space and is hatched in the diagrams on this page.
2. If a hatched patch so defined is similarly surrounded by other hatched patches, then it turns cross-hatched (Y-Y-Y-Y space).

In the images then, white is the one cell size open space, hatched the two cell deep, cross-hatched three cells deep and so on.

This begins to differentiate the spatial system, and points the way to an emergent superstructure for the otherwise locally defined spatial organisation. They appear to be spread quite evenly throughout the system, and in the more constrained systems (high closed space ratios as in the zoomed examples) appear at the centre of growing pods of space. Thus from a simple universal rule we can observe globally differentiated spatial organisation, which could form the basis for second and third order processes.

The global form can also be seen as the outcome of the deviation amplifying coupling between open and closed space, and on the next two pages some examples are shown in more detail.

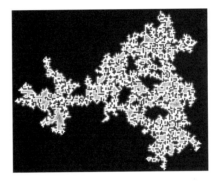

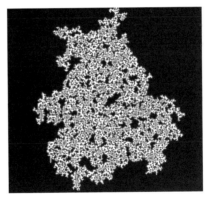

Example of second and third order observations on the spatial configuration

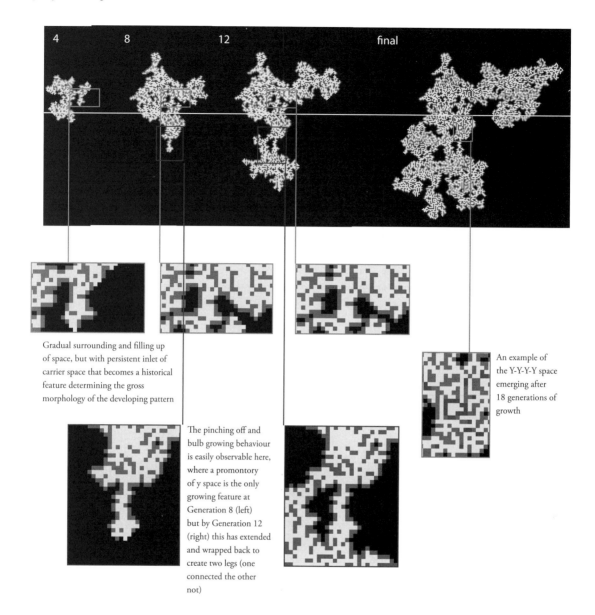

Gradual surrounding and filling up of space, but with persistent inlet of carrier space that becomes a historical feature determining the gross morphology of the developing pattern

The pinching off and bulb growing behaviour is easily observable here, where a promontory of y space is the only growing feature at Generation 8 (left) but by Generation 12 (right) this has extended and wrapped back to create two legs (one connected the other not)

An example of the Y-Y-Y-Y space emerging after 18 generations of growth

A dynamic model of the growth of San'a

San'a is the capital of the Yemen, and has long been recognised as an archetypical example of the urban morphology of the region. In the last century a number of European geographers and urbanists studied the town (e.g. Varanda (1982), Sallma (1992) and Kaizer (1984)), and in conversation with local representatives, my student Ali Khudair was able to establish something of the social and political history of San'a and other Yemeni settlements.

The conventional approach to studying the architectural morphology of such a settlement as evidenced by many books on the subject (Cullen (1961) and Lynch (1960)) is to rely on a global description of the morphology and try to fit the social dynamics on to it. For instance, much is often made of the role of early sultans and princes, and the role of the church and state is emphasised in founding buildings and defining planning rules and regulations. Similarly ,since the topic was subsumed under 'urban design', the 1960's 'townscape' movement (articles published in *Architectural Review* 1965–69) relied on the aesthetic assessment of the observed morphology rather than attempting to explain why it was there in the first place.

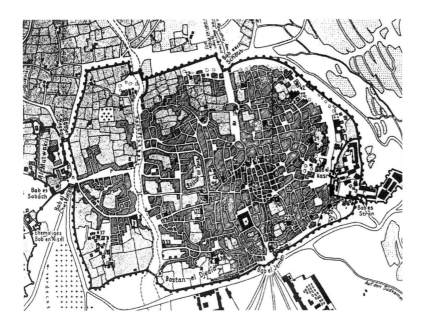

San'a's morphology

(*above*) Plan

(*below*) Examples of four types of morphology in San'a:

1. Bostan (Garden) between the wall and an incursion of houses.
2. The central souk area of tight spaces
3. Unbuilt land next to a road
4. Traditional Bostan surrounded by houses

1   2   3   4

Relationship with the previous model

In the earlier discussion it was seen that in some values for the proportion of x space to y space, the growing configuration developed 'holes' of carrier space. This points out the way that these bostans (gardens) can be seen as emergent properties of the system. While the global structure of the two-state automaton is less convincing than the three state CA described next, this model could be seen as the general underlying case. It is important to find the underlying behaviours of such models before we start explicitly specifying them, but to uncover what may, after all, be already built into the topological necessities of the system. In view of this underlying structure, it was decided to develop the CA version of the model rather than the DLA version described above.

The morphology of San'a and other traditional Yemeni towns has many similarities to that described by the turn-taking Alpha Syntax, but differs in the same way as the parallel version: the existence of large inaccessible garden areas behind the houses, often in association with mosques and whose ownership is essentially God's, i.e. it does not belong to anyone, but the mosque looks after it. These green areas are used for the production of food and often have communal wells, and in the discussion below are referred to as gardens. However, it must be remembered that individual houses are not paired up with individual bits of garden, but simply abut the communal open area. It must also be remembered that describing the areas as communal does not imply that the houses bordering the garden have either individual access or rights to the land.

Where the gardens exist then the basic syntax can be extended thus:

- road > road;
- house > road;
- garden > house;
- garden > garden.

So instead of the (Y > Y / X > Y) syntax, we have essentially a Y > X > Y syntax, with the second Y representing the gardens. Otherwise the syntax is the same as for the Alpha Syntax above. That is, gardens are usually behind houses, not directly attached to roads, but houses are also built without gardens. It is also possible to observe roads next to gardens without houses (see detail 3 of the image opposite) and this can be achieved in the model by relaxing some of the more rigorous exclusions of the rules set out below.

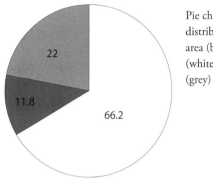

Pie chart showing the distribution of built area (black), roads (white) and gardens (grey)

The San'a model then is a three-state CA, where the state change rules are of two types:

1. a change from unoccupied to either garden, house or road;
2. a change from any of the occupied types to any other.

The algorithm

NetLogo provides facilities for building CA using patches (small square cells which can be given variables and behaviours) and neighbour counting functions for summing the totals of patches' variables in either the Moore (nsum4) or von Neumann (nsum) neighbourhood.

The San'a algorithm uses both neighbourhoods. These values are used in the state change rules which are as follows:

1. The general case of putting a garden 'behind' a house – if a cell is empty and has exactly one house in the nsum4 count, or there is more than one garden in the nsum4 count and there are no roads in the nsum count, then turn the patch into a garden.
2. Extend garden area beyond houses – if a cell is empty and there are more than two gardens in the nsum count, then turn the patch into a garden.
3. Make roads and houses – if a cell is empty and there are some roads near and less than two gardens, then on the flip of a coin set it to either road or house.

And two tidying up rules:

4. Houses demoted to roads – if a cell is a house and there is a road and no other houses in the big neighbourhood and less than four garden cells, then the house become a road.
5. Gardens become houses – if the cell is a garden with some neighbouring roads, then it becomes a house.

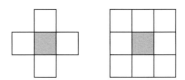

Nsum4 and Nsum neighbourhood

If pc = 0 and courthouse = 1 or courtgarden > 1 and countroadbig = 0 [setgarden 1 setroad 0 sethouse 0]

If pc = 0 and countgardenbig > 2 [setgarden 1 setroad 0 sethouse 0]

If pc = 0 and countroad > 0 and countgarden < 2 chose randomly 50:50 between

if house = 1 and count road = 1 and courthouse = 0 and courthousebig >0 and countgardenbig < 4

if garden = 1 and countroad >0

As in the simple two state CA, the state change from unoccupied to road or house can also be modified by altering the probability that an unoccupied cell will change into a house or a road. The sequence below illustrates the gross morphology of structures using values of X (house) probabilities from 20% to 90%.

High probability

20%	30%	40%	50%

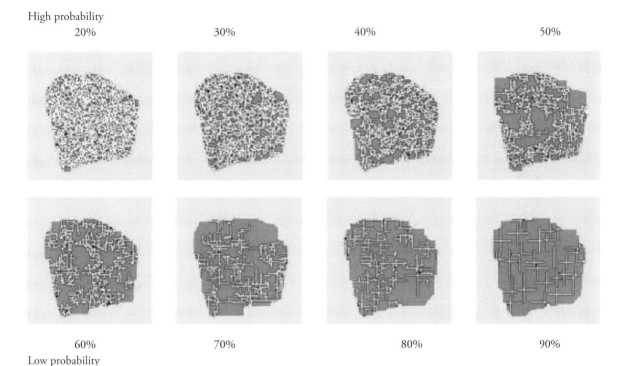

60%	70%	80%	90%

Low probability

Variations of morphology with differing probabilities

It can be observed that, as the probability that an unoccupied cell which is a candidate for change will turn into a road approaches 100%, the overall morphology becomes more street like and the area of garden increases. With low probabilities the morphology is granular and Alpha Syntax like, with minimal gardens. Comparing the actual proportions of garden to road/house in the real San'a shows that 50:50 is probably about right for replicating the observed morphology.

Seeding

Town gates

Roads

Roads and squares

Scatter

From top to bottom, seeding with town gates, roads, roads and squares, and scatter

Seeding conditions

In all runs of the CA, the initial state must be seeded with at least one piece of road space in order for the algorithm to work. There are a number of possibilities, all of which are easily explored:

- a single seed somewhere;
- a scattering of seeds; and
- seeding from particular globally defined access points or targets (roads etc.).

Also, the developing pattern can either be constrained (by defining some arbitrary boundary to growth) or limited to the rectangular border of the calowed to wrap round as on a 3D torus (the conventional life game scenario).

In order to study the effects of the arbitrary limit to growth, a 'town wall' was defined in the final experiments, and it could be observed that this provided a way of filling in and of consolidation at the borders that led to more natural global effects than the boundless versions where the natural effect of all Cellular Automata to become everywhere homogeneous. As well as the (trivial) cosmetic effect, therefore, the boundary condition provides feedback which differentiates the edges from the middle. The relative probabilities for X/Y (house/road) are the same for all examples at 50:50.

Seeding with town gates

The small white blobs at the top left right and bottom are set to be road stuff, and the result is four systems of space developing out from these positions. No development can be initiated in the centre. At the settings for road/house probabilities, the developing spatial configuration of X and Y space blocks itself before covering the area.

Seeding with roads and square

The linear elements have been added to the blobs, so that the emergent surface can begin anywhere along the lines drawn in white, which of course leads to a more even spread, but still less coverage than observed in San'a.

Seeding with scatter

Randomly positioned white patches are used as the initial generators, with no linear or edge patches set. The development covers the area more evenly with a better match to San'a's bostans in size and distribution.

Studies of traditional Yemeni family structure and historical development seemed to indicate that the initial stages of the development of a settlement consisted of a number of unconnected family encampments that slowly coagulated over time. This favoured the random scatter seeding, rather than the growth from the town gates and market square options.

In all but the scatter examples, the gardens tended to be too big and disproportionately situated around the edges of the expanding road/house network.

Discussion

The only claim that is made for the San'a algorithm is its compactness, and the generalised ability to develop agglomerations of three states with a wide range of morphologies. Obviously the strictly orthogonal grid of the CA makes it impossible to model the actual widths and areas of streets and houses, so good matches with actual ratios can only be approximated.

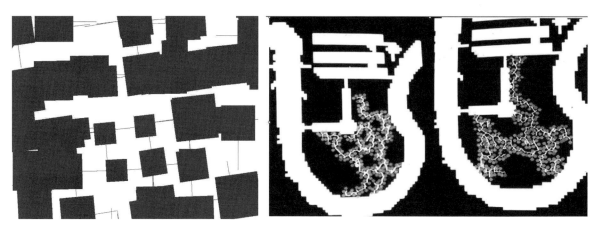

The Alpha Syntax off the grid in its various guises
The Isle of Dogs images on the right were early Pascal/GEM implementations

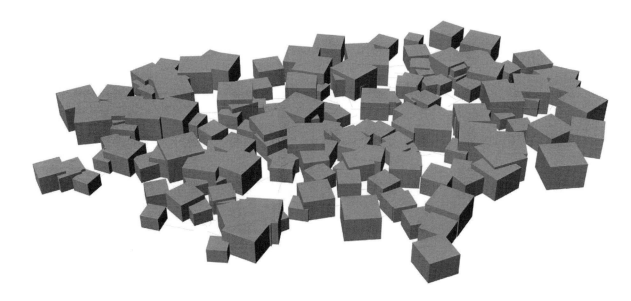

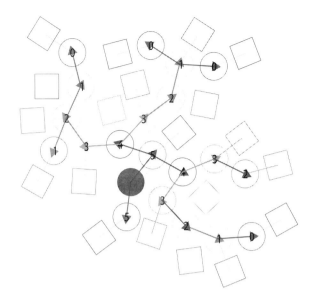

The progress of the algorithm (which counts backwards from the seed space (disc) from 5 to 0 in the illustration above). The numbers in the circles are the recursion value of the successive Y spaces, so 5 links to 4, which links to 3, 2, 1, 0 and so on. Once the recursion bottoms out it unwinds back, trying to add more nodes as it unfolds until all avenues have been explored and it ends back where it started. In this algorithm it is slightly more difficult to check for planarity (the developing network may not cross itself) and to avoid building on top of an existing cell. In the cellular versions it was only necessary to inspect a cell to check if it was occupied, here we need to search the developing model to check for intersections. In the illustrations on the left, some overlapping has been allowed for the sake of variety.

The new vernacular – deep structure of the picturesque

Alpha Syntax off the grid

All the examples of generated spatial systems shown so far are based on a rigid cellular array of square boxes which all have four face-joining neighbours and eight altogether. In order to provide a less geometrically constrained model, the Alpha Syntax model 'off the grid' (was developed in Pascal on a Commodore Pet 8-bit micro. Subsequently this was transferred to the Dec 10 – the advanced successor to the old ICL machine at Liverpool Polytechnic. A version was also converted to run on the PC under GEM – an early precursor to Windows (screenshots opposite)). Removing the cellular constraints not only allows for more flexible geometry, but also for a wider range of topologies. As the grid is free of orthogonal constraints, X and Y spaces can be different sizes from each other (small houses, big roads), and also houses and road elements can be randomly different sizes as well. The resulting configuration is a network, made up of:

1. a branching tree structure of Y space, starting from the initial seed; and
2. a set of 'leaves' of X space.

How it works

The general idea is of a branching tree structure in 2D which is forced to be planar (there are no bridges or underground passages). The first thing is to start with the seed cell, here drawn as a circle. This is the origin of the open space system. After that new Y spaces (circles) are added as long as they can be associated with a new X space (square). The angle and size of the spaces are dependent on the parameters for a particular run of the system. This goes on until the stipulated number of recursions have elapsed and/or no more spaces can be added.

A series of runs with the number of angles set to 4 and a range
of sizes from 1 to 10 on the left to 9 to 10 on the right

A series of runs with the number of angles set to 100 and a
range of sizes from 1 to 10 on the left to 9 to 10 on the right

Morphological outcomes of varying geometry and/or topology

The model has four main parameters which control the geometry and topology of the growing spatial system.

The sequence of images on the left show the variety of global outcomes that are achieved by varying some of the parameters. The top row uses four angles (roughly equivalent to the orthogonal grid), but varying the range of possible sizes for x and y spaces, where x is the black box and y is the grey circle from large range (1 to 10) to small range (9 to 10 – spaces are nearly all the same size). As the range of sizes decreases, the agglomeration becomes more open and extended, with a variety of different open space types and many rings and circuits providing multiple routes through the spatial system.

The same thing can be seen in the lower example, but here the possible angle is unconstrained. In this case the overall morphology becomes more free form as you would of course expect.

Generally with most spaces being the same size, a street-like geometry emerges; with the larger ranges of size, the spatial system is more varied with mostly interconnected space with islands of buidlings in the middle.

The large image in the middle is shaded to reflect the level of recursion – the history of the development where light equals early and dark equals late. This is the same information as shown in the numbered diagram on the previous page. Inevitably early development is in the central part of the system, but over time development folds back into the centre and multiple 'places' develop with a clear morphogenetic feedback – the history of the development influences later growth patterns.

These are purely abstract outcomes, but it is possible to map the geometry of the system to actual agglomerations seen in vernacular settlements. For instance, a varied range of sizes implies a mix of uses and requirements. To the extent that very extreme settings for the parameters to the system result in very compact systems could be taken to explain the varying sizes and grain of settlements – as observed in the wild, as it were.

The illustrations on the left, which are of course taken from the Alpha Syntax generative model, are offered as a comment on the idea of the vernacular. The overall shape and size of spatial configuration is posited as a 'natural' response to the fact of human occupation of the land, and that any attempt to 'design' such an outcome is, at best, to impose some quaint idea of the picturesque, or at worst the imposition of over-simplified regimented housing with little variety, designed by persons other than the inhabitants.

So who designed the images here? Of course it was authored by whoever wrote the software, and whoever chose the views and manipulated the images. The actual vernacular settlements have thus been absorbed and modelled as a process, and now have been disgorged in a simulation. The role of the designer has been turned into one of defining abstract principles of agglomeration, and any particular outcome, such as the one pictured, can be seen as just an example of what sort of thing might happen if such a process were allowed to occur in the physical world.

The algorithmic approach, and in particular deviation amplifying agglomerative process modelling, lends itself to the formation of a synthetic vernacular, where the architecture slowly accumulates and reflects the notion of variations on a theme, complicatedness and self-similarity, amid a succession of unique spatial events.

This chapter is intended to answer a general point about the use of algorithms as descriptions of socially defined space and the submerged nine-tenths of the built environment, as opposed to the more architectural examples in the previous chapters.

The image on the left attempts to render the generated spatial system as an homage to Gordon Cullen, who throughout the 1960s published many articles in the *Architectural Review* which culminated in the definition of something called 'Townscape'.

The quality of space, with its unfolding vistas and 'glimpses' of spaces connected to the one you are standing in, can be synthesised by a virtual camera positioned in the Alpha Syntax agglomeration. The circles on the ground are the Y space symbols, left in so as not to imply (despite the pencil Photoshop rendering) that this is anything other than a fake.

chapter six

Epilogue or rethinking representation (again)

The previous chapters have attempted to set out the idea that the generative algorithm is a sufficient representation of spatial organisation/morphology.

This book has tried to set out a few puzzles that surround the world of computers and space/form. It attempts to give a flavour of the discussions and methodologies that have been around for many years. We start from the latest approaches to the subject in Chapter 1, where we look at the structure and methods of distributed representation, the idea of the emergent consensus. This covers the whole idea of self-organization, a mostly post-modern take on morphology which tries to avoid making simplistic assumptions about meaning, information and geometry. Following on from this, the book works its way back to classical approaches to form generation using production systems and evolutionary grammars of form.

All the time the text of the algorithm is presented as a common thread that unifies these disparate approaches to form and spatial configuration, and hopefully provides a platform for understanding.

The most common discussion I hope is about the status of the observer in these models, and the need to try always to avoid tautology when building them. Gordon Pask's edict that we have to ensure an epistemic independence of the model from the structure of the outcome is about the idea that the code does not directly generate the patterns observed in a simple one-to-one correspondence, but that this comes out of the process itself with its feedback loops and reflexivity.

The discussion of spiders, robots and boids in the middle of the book is intended to show how there is a subtle relationship between our ideas of consciousness and what we observe either in natural systems or computer simulations. This can lead to some quite difficult places, but I personally like the idea of tackling notions of intuition and hunch, which many creative people feel is so important. 'Hello world' is the recognition that we, as coders, are also consumers of our work with machines.

Getting back to the nuts and bolts, the chapter on the use of Lindemayer systems and genetic programming is an attempt to present some actual languages that can represent form, and to cover the rich history of symbolic notation. The last section on distributed models of urban aggregation and the presentation of a couple of canonical algorithms, especially the pond slime model, is intended to wrap up the discussion on representation, taking us back to the foundations of cybernetics and 'deviation amplifying' mutual causalities, which finally may include consideration of the most important aspect of architecture – human occupation and encounter in spatial systems.

What are the implications of this?

We are not insisting on asserting that the algorithm is the only or best description, but at least trying to point out (and de-mystify) the idea that there is something 'there' underneath/behind the image that is not maths and equations (which are always made up summaries of processes), but a good/appropriate description of the process at work to generate the observed outcome. Before the invention of the general purpose automatic symbol processor – the Turing machine or 'computer' – very clever people spent their time compressing their observations on long and complicated processes into the shortest pithyest statement they could manage, simply because the only technology they possessed was a pencil and paper. As a non-mathematician, I have been aware that 'using the computer' is seen by real mathematicians as a very third class way of behaving, yet I understand that, for instance, they have yet to capture the essence of fluid dynamics for instance.

I have to admit that the general position of this book is structuralist in nature, partly due to a heavy dependence on the thoughts of Bill Hillier, and of course on the use of artificial language and Chomsky's generative scheme as a model for form production. The phrase used in the last chapter, 'the deep structure of the picturesque', is deliberately provocative in that it conjoins two old, but still useful, projects into one. Perhaps the massive wave of the cultural studies people has passed somewhat, leaving a few survivors twitching in the sand to plod on in this very English pursuit of philosophy in the tradition of the logical positivists, the structuralists, and an interest in the natural language of architecture.

While the interest in the vernacular seems to propose the death of the author, the focus on the new text of the algorithm suggests a new author, the architect as systems designer, a person who can define spatial organisation and form as systems of feedback and morphogenesis cast in the form of instructions to a Turing machine. This new author can learn from at least 150 years of experiment and argument about design that has lead to the gradual acceptance of the ideas of systems in morphogenesis and design.

In the library of the Architectural Association (AA) there are a number of vast tomes entitled *The Grammar of Ornament* (1856) by Owen Jones (1809–74). The use of the word grammar in this case is clearly not to be conflated with structuralist or post-structuralist ideas of language, but simply an arbitrary artificial set of rules for structuring and classifying the decorative arts of the previous two millennia. Grammar for this Victorian gent was thought of as a categorising scheme, whose origins lay in the grammars of Latin, and the general concept of the grammar school, which implies that a grammar is a settled set of rules for ordering the artificial language of human beings. However, in true modern manner, the authority for a grammar is given not by antiquity, but by a set of 37 propositions (such as No. 8, 'All ornament should be based on a geometrical construction').

He hoped that rather than slavishly copying the exact examples illustrated, people would, as a consequence of the book, begin to understand the laws of ornament as adumbrated in the 37 propositions and illustrated in the plates, and generate their own decorations. Owen was insistent that in order to be beautiful, ornament had to derive from the world of nature ('whenever any style of ornament commands universal admiration, it will always be found to be in accordance with the laws which regulate the distribution of form in nature').

This book has attempted to illuminate a small corner of what used to be known as design methodology. Design method is an explicification of designing, a bringing out into the open, making explicit, of what is otherwise implicit or tacit. Schools of design have always had to balance the need to let students have their creative heads with some attempt at codification and discipline. If you set up an academy it is necessary to be academic, and to do that you need a theory of design. Without a theory you may as well just rely on the old articled apprenticeship method which assumes that:

- we will continue to do things in much the same way that we always have; and
- nothing is going to change.

Design methodology was not invented by architects, but by engineers and operational research scientists. The engineers (mechanical rather than civil) could properly use the twin simplifications of having an objective statement of the operational capabilities of the thing to be designed, and a rational way of calculating the cost of the project. The goal of design method was to optimise between maximising capabilities and minimising cost.

Refinements have been made to both the way of defining the capabilities (a good engineer will know that there are many possible solutions to a given set of delivery targets) and costs (environmental impact, social and life costs, etc.), but the fundamental idea remains that an optimum can be defined. This has always been a problem for architecture, where the incommensurability of many classes of functional criteria prevents easy optimisation.

However, it is possible to theorise the production of buildings without concerning oneself with epistemological problems of how to define goodness and truth in design, by just concentrating on the way that designs are communicated between all the people involved in the building process. As the great industrial enterprises of the nineteenth century developed, new ways of managing the actors were developed and Taylorism, the measurement of time and motion, came to be applied as 'scientific management'. Ideas of productivity, which were developed for the steel mills of 1890's Pennsylvania, came to be applied to the planning and layout of machinery, and by analogy to domestic kitchens where the goal of equipment layout was to reduce the number of miles the average housewife trudged between the cooker and the sink. In terms of spatial layout, this approach held out the possibility of optimal arrangements of equipment and human movement.

Design as management

This paradigm of design was based on the idea that designing generally was a matter of solving a large number of conflicting operations in order to work out the best procedure to tackle the overall task. This approach was (and is) called Operational Research (OR). The computer was seen as a once only machine for sorting this out, in the best 1940's manner. This view of design (we already know how to do all the bits, we just have to think about the order we are going to do them) is essentially a manager's view, but it was eventually applied to architectural design, since that too was seen as predominantly a management task. This view fits in well with the computer-aided design (CAD) vendors and large practices' view of design.

Logic models of design

As part of the computer-aided architectural design (CAAD) industry, and in an attempt to bring the management of design contracts into line with the management of construction generally (which is a part of the overall management procedures referred to above as OR), a number of researchers have developed OR models of what goes on in the design task. This management view of design is principally concerned with the structuring of the many sub-tasks in a design, and while it offers a way out for bad managers, does not impinge directly on the contemplation of the sub-tasks or help in deciding what to do in the first place.

Design as problem solving

The original model for design methodology was borrowed from the top-down analytical methods derived from the enlightenment, where the overall idea was that what was going on was finding out a puzzle using one's intellect. The method is to start with the big problem, and break it down into smaller ones, until you find one you can easily solve, then clamber back up the tree of problems until you have reached the top when all sub-problems are solved. The way of solving a problem is to express it in a formal language (classically mathematics), after which the solution will 'fall' out automatically. Basically this is a good system, but it depends crucially on everyone agreeing what the problem is in the first place and how to test solutions. The early proponents of artificial intelligence used a logic formalism called predicate calculus which allowed the expression of such facts as:

> Bob is the father of Jim;
> Jim is the father of Alice,
> and allowed for asking
> Is Bob the grandfather of Alice?

The bible of the mathematical approach for architecture was March and Steadman's *The Geometry of Environment* (1970), which covered ways of representing plans, reports on theorems for establishing the enumeration of patterns, properties of symmetry and many others. It is necessary, before embarking on any methodological attempt to design, to have a way of representing the components as you, the designer, conceptualise them. Take, for instance, the plan. One of the properties of the plan is the way in which the various rooms are connected. March and Steadman showed how three apparently different plan ideas of Frank Lloyd Wright, based on circles, squares and triangles, were identical if you just considered the graph of what is connected to what. Thus the core ideas in the book were necessary groundwork for a lot of the top-down design method research of the 1960s and 1970s, providing the methodology for a wide range of studies, including the planning examples referred to below. At the same time, Christopher Alexander's *A City is Not A Tree* (subtitle – 'It's a Semi-lattice') (1965) used the network analogy to describe the difference between hierarchical organisation and more distributed networks, as part of his general critique of top-down central planning and preference for bottom-up organisation. In 1966 Stanford Anderson gave a talk at the AA entitled 'Problem Solving = Problem Worrying'. The main thrust of his talk was to demolish the then fashionable notion that the design of a building could be undertaken as a linear rational enterprise, starting from the problem definition and

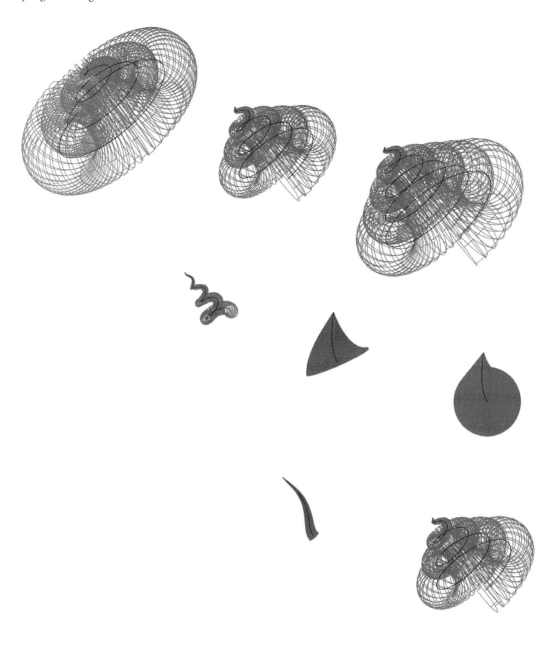

Some spirals generated in the course of an evolutionary
session by Hawry Khalid, a student on MSc Computing and
Design, University of London, 2003

ending in the solution – a building whose function was perfectly suited to the problem statement. He suggested that, in reality, the process was more likely to be one of 'problem worrying', where a cycle of problem definition, partial solution and redefinition was always necessary. This was/is because:

- it is impossible to define all the problems that an architectural object has to solve; and
- the production of an actual morphology (attempt at a 'building') feeds back on the initial problem statement because any proposal will entail originally unintended consequences.

The reciprocity of form and program

An early example of problem solving which demonstrates the pitfalls of this approach is the automatic planning software (written in Fortran and distributed as a pack of punched cards) that was written in the late 1960s. The algorithm was as follows:

1. Develop a table of relationships between all the rooms (or for a more abstract representation, the activities) in the proposed building.
2. In the cells of the table (think spreadsheet), put a number whose value represents the strength of connection demanded between the two activities.
3. The goal is to rearrange the table by swapping rows and columns until a calculation of each cell value multiplied by its distance from the diagonal (a kind of moments about a point equation) reaches a minimum.
4. Once the matrix/table has settled down, reading along the top of the table the now rearranged spaces/activities labels will be in order of optimum relationship, starting from the middle outwards.
5. Working from the middle outwards of this list, and taking account of the actual size of the spaces, plot out the plan arrangement.

Now, the problem was that it rather depended on how you defined the relationship between the circulation and the spaces as to how the plan came out. If you did the obvious (circulation is connected to everything), then the circulation would end up in the middle of the plan, which was inconvenient as it did not allow a way into the building. The other thing was that it turned out that planning was not considered a

difficult thing to do by architects. Many refinements were added, with multiple matrices, better sorting and ranking algorithms, and so on. Versions of these were taken up by circuitboard layout designers and have become standard practice, but architects, who had a very much richer set of tools to use in constructing the layout (mode of construction, types of space, occupation), found that the results were unhelpful. In fact, the difference between circuitboard layout and building plans is a good example of the fundamental difference between clear, objective engineering constraints and aims (components are absolutely defined, tracks predetermined, and the goal is to reduce the length of the tracks and nothing else) and their architectural equivalents, which are less clearly defined.

Failings of the inductive method

Anderson pointed out that design optimisation operations, such as those described in Chapter 4, were examples of induction (as opposed to the goal-seeking methods of logic programming described above). Induction starts with a collection of facts or observations from which arise some common overarching organisational principle. This inference (as opposed to deduction) can be supported by the mechanics of logic in strictly scientific induction, or just be 'obvious'. He presents the use of any design method as a form of 'justification', as a way of taking the heat off the designer by resolving the problem into a check list which, if all the boxes are ticked, can be justified as a 'good solution'.

Rather than seeking a clearly defined goal (the first justificational approach), this second justificational approach is <u>inductive</u>, seeking to define the problem carefully in order to have a fixed standard against which to judge any proposed problem solution.

Thus, this whole approach can be criticised in at least two serious ways:

1. the usual problem of inductivist theories that they can never be sure that they have adequate data from which to synthesise, or even adequate data to check against, if one is seeking justification; and
2. that the process of creative design is artificially simplified in order that it may be viewed more

systematically and in order that its results may be justified by their consistency with an initial statement.

This, even though the original statement may be a curious artefact that bears only slight resemblance to the new problem situation.

Natural (analogue) computing

There are examples of inductive morphological systems that do not use computers, the best known being the work of Frei Otto (Stuttgart Institute for Lightweight structures), where his generative systems used natural materials (string, glue, water, soap, films, gravity) and other forces to 'calculate' optimally shaped objects. The upside-down catenary models of Gaudi, which he used to calculate the angles and vaults for the sloping columns of the Sagrada Familia, are also good examples of 'natural computing'.

Natural computing was essential in the past as it allowed designers to experiment with the use of massively parallel computations going on in sand piles, soap bubbles, interconnected systems of weights and tensile supports, and so on. It is a consequence of the new computational models, such as Cellular Automata, that the natural world is seen as an emergent outcome of parallel computation. This is an example of choosing to observe the world in a new light, based on a new epistemology.

The use of computers has allowed an attempt to take on board the criticisms of the inductive method, using the computer as a way of 'discovering structure through an interesting situation of multiple conjectures and criticism', a quote Stanford takes from William Bartley's work. Thus the anti-inductivist model leads directly to the pursuit of evolutionary algorithms and the mimicking of natural processes by the computer to explore problem spaces on a trial and error basis. Nature's dictum could be summed up as: 'better luck next time'.

The book has attempted to demonstrate ways in which this evolutionary, suck it and see, artificial life approach to problem solving is best served by using the computer, to worry at problems much as a puppy will worry his prey. The examples given in Chapter 2 of Cellular

Image of shells

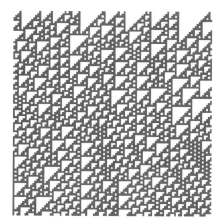

1D CA generated with NetLogo

Automata outlined the general mechanisms at work. A good example of this new way of looking is the patterns on the shell (above). The organisation of the pattern into repeated different sized triangular regions is more or less the same as certain outcomes of running a one-dimensional Cellular Automaton (Wolfram, 2002). The Cellular Automaton consists of a single line of cells (black or white) which can be imagined as stretching across the top of a piece of paper. The rules for the Cellular Automaton are of the type where each cell in this line checks the ones either side of it to determine what colour it should change to. The next generation is drawn below the current run so the lines of black and white cells are drawn successively down the page. With many of the possible 256 rules, the shell pattern emerges. This would indicate that the shell is growing a new line of cells on its growing edge, using some type of diffusion process which is mimicked by the one-dimensional Cellular Automaton. The system can also be modelled in terms of complex systems of non-linear simultaneous equations, and is often presented thus in academic papers, but the Cellular Automaton model seems to be more natural and considerably simpler. However, the traditional mathematical approach still has greater academic prestige, and is used in preference to the simpler explanation – yet another example of the dead hand of Victorian mathematics at work!

Parallelism allows us to explore the real world where things happen simultaneously, in particular the world of material stuff, which emerges as a shape we can observe. Setting up such experiments provides a mechanism for observing the effects of many individual actions which, when acted on in parallel, demonstrate some observable outcomes that seem to be defined globally, i.e. they can be recognised by our perceptual systems as 'interesting' or patterned.

The point is that there are hardly any things in the natural world (Dawkins, 1996) whose form/shape are the products of a simple linear morphological process. On the contrary, they all seem to be the result of lots of things happening at once. This is not surprising because the world is essentially made up of lots and lots of things which act at the same time as each other, and many morphologies arise by the way the multiple things interact with each other simultaneously over time.

In other words, the way we design and make shapes is most unnatural, since it depends on a 'one thing at a time' way of working. Our linear approach to thinking (determined by our inability to think of more than one thing at a time, or at least to be conscious of thinking, since of course our mental processes are actually the emergent property of typical parallel behaviour of all the billions of neurones in our brains) has been mirrored by the von Neumann machine (computer) which can also only do one thing at a time. So it is difficult to imagine how we can model/replicate/test and generally experiment with the parallel morphogenesis taking place all around us using computers.

With advances in computers it is possible to create a virtual parallel machine so that we can experiment with parallel morphogenesis. In order to do so we have to reorder our thoughts from the global to the local, and

to define algorithms to drive the processes in the virtual world. One of the encouraging things is that it turns out that, although there are many processes going on at the same time, they are *all the same*. This was discussed in Chapters 1 and 2; sufficient to say here that the key thing is that, while such systems consist of many similar small programs executing in parallel, each one has a different relationship to all the others. Even in systems which only deal with immediate neighbours, your view of the neighbours will differ from their view of you, if the initial set-up contains any irregularities. Similarly, the view from below may be uniform, but the view from above will be global. Consider the 'Mexican Wave' as observed at football grounds; as far as the participants are concerned, they are all doing the same thing, which is to lift up their arms once a sufficient number of people around them have also done so. From the other side of the stadium, however, it appears that a great wave of hands is travelling along the stands – this is the global outcome of the local process which is observable by the global observer, not any one person in the stands themselves.

Design as search

The general case in this approach is to conceptualise the business of designing something as a process of trying things out until you come across a thing that satisfies your design intentions (however defined). There is an underlying assumption that sometimes you will stumble across this good solution; otherwise the whole journey would not be worth the candle. In order to go from one not very good solution to another slightly better solution, it is necessary to formalise the task of defining the operations that make up the design process. If the many operations are set out, we can see them as parameters of some process (like numbers or any other enumerable type) and so the search can be seen as a journey through a mathematical 'space' whose dimensions are as numerous as the number of parameters to the problem. Spaces with more dimensions than three are difficult to visualise, but after all these are metaphors. The main thing such spaces have in common with true spaces is that increasing the number of dimensions of a problem increases the size of the search space geometrically. Using automatic search algorithms (i.e. computing the space) will speed things up, but this increase in size for all but trivial problems means that other techniques are needed to get a useful result in finite time.

If the many dimensions of the design task are seen as the locations of pre-existent possible designs, then how can we track them down?

Enumeration

In the 1970s in England, a number of researchers based at Cambridge University embarked on a series of exhaustive enumeration studies of rectangular tessellations, which basically meant conventional floorplans made up of differently proportioned rectangles, which conformed to arbitrary rules about usefulness (not too long and thin, basically) and had to pack into a simple rectangular plan. It will be evident that such objects are principally layouts for simple houses, and the underlying idea was to explore all the possibilities using a computer in the hope that it would turn up 'something interesting'. The idea was that such interesting/appropriate plans would be missed by human designers because they would not have the time to work through all the combinations. The number of different solutions to the problem increased exponentially, with nine rooms generating many thousands of results.

These algorithms used a number of key representations, referred to above in reference to Steadman and March – principally the network analogy for diagramming the relationship between rooms in a building, also used in space planning algorithms. The basic problem with exhaustive search is that it produces too many examples, and tends to generate an expanding number of solutions, which need to be analysed after the event – another whole can of worms.

To cut down on the number of possible solutions, it was decided to weed out unlikely arrangements by developing higher order syntax for the way things can be put together. These 'shape grammars' were there to reduce the population of solutions by culling ungrammatical solutions, and then only developing those that passed. William Fawcett, in his book *Architecture: A Formal Approach* (1990), shows how a restricted grammar can be used to generate a smaller range of likely designs, and the Genetic Programming section in Chapter 4 indicated a way this approach can be abstracted still further, from the use of handwritten rules to generated rules.

Parallel search

As was pointed out in the earlier discussion about natural computing and the digital equivalent, morphogenesis is always (in the natural world) the result of the cumulative effect of many parallel computations. While this phenomenon is thus demonstrated to arrive at some conclusion or other, it needs further refinement to enable it to search the space of all possible designs. Principally, each processor has to agree with the others about how to partition up the job, and the answer currently is to start by searching at random, and then apply a test to see how everybody is going on, then set everyone off randomly again, but this time from the most promising location. This is of course the *evolutionary algorithm*. It cuts down the time needed to reach a solution, the many parallel strands converging quickly onto one part of the search space, having collectively agreed to ignore other areas. Evolutionary algorithms suffer from the same problem as all such optimisation procedures, that of having to define a fitness function – the evaluation test that determines who survives each generation.

With all design-space search algorithms there are two decisions to be taken, both of which restrict the applicability of the approach. The dimensionality of the search space is determined by the number of parameters to the problem, and the direction taken within those dimensions is determined by the fitness function. In *Climbing Mount Improbable*, Richard Dawkins (1996) uses the shell as an example of a simple system of three parameters, which define a cubic search space (conveniently illustratable with a 3D diagram). The basic mechanism is a spirally growing tube, the parameters are flare (the expansion rate of the spiral), spire (the degree to which it extends perpendicular to the plane of rotation) and verm (how much the tube gets bigger as it grows).

What is interesting is that not all positions in the 'shell design space' are occupied, the shaded areas represent the positions of the major families of shells, but being in the world, and being made of particular stuff, some combinations are just too fragile, unwieldy or no good for houses/horns.

Design as emergent phenomena

The two main ways of looking at how designing is done are summarised as 'top-down' and 'bottom-up'. Standard problem-solving is mostly top-down, and evolutionary strategies are mostly bottom-up. The top-down approach assumes we know what the problem is as a whole, we just need to find out what the components are; the bottom-up approach assumes we can define the low-level components of some problem, we just do not know how they can be combined to form a solution.

The truly bottom-up approach sees the design as not just the result of a parallel evolutionary search in the search space, but a creative act which actually constructs a new search space in order for the design to fit into it.

The use of computers to explore emergent form has one advantage in that, in order to build the morphological system, you have to define it in a formal language (define an algorithm) which brings the structure and meaning of the model proposed into the realms of expression and debate (and also conveniently allows it to be programmed for automatic execution). This use of formal languages in modelling should provide a basis for the development of a theory of form and shape, which has more chance of being adopted and discussed than the conventional discursive art historical method because all the underlying assumptions are clearly laid out, not hidden by conventional approaches and the nineteenth-century idea of creativity.

So to summarise the summary:

> *Essentially the generative models shown in this book are used to develop patterns of spatial organisation, patterns of solid and void; in the most basic case, just lines on paper, marks on the screen.*

And what this book is saying is:

> *A corridor/village/dom-ino house is what you get when you run this piece of code here.*

This is what Marvin Minsky is saying about the difference between a program to check your theory and a program that *is* your theory.

In the case of the village (urban space system), this point was reached after the initial generative studies were done at University College London 20 years ago, as described in the preceding chapter. What eventually became 'space syntax' was the development of tools for measuring and comparing the output from the generative model with actual spaces, and then to measure spaces found in the world.

So we write a program to analyse space, we employ roomfuls of PhD students to develop tools for measuring, and we build up an impressive portfolio of cases. After this we can perhaps say that we have 'proved' that the analysis of space provides us with a way of predicting people movement in that space.

However, the original idea, that the generative model could be used to develop patterns of spatial organisation, gets lost in this case – the code is just checking, not being the theory.

How does the code describe the pattern? It does not take a global view and measure it, as you might find yourself doing by just looking at the output (looks like a 'beady ring' as Hillier is fond of saying of the Alpha Syntax models). It is a description of a process, usually a simple process. The code is, as we have tried to show, independent of the outcome (the epistemic autonomy idea) – it does not 'know' what is going to happen, just as the DNA in an organism does not 'know' that it is going to grow two legs. (And the neurons in my brain do not know what I am thinking about!) The distributed representation means that the pattern is not coded anywhere, but everywhere.

In terms of architecture and its relation to human occupation there is one mapping that we could make, especially in terms of the village and agglomerative morphologies generally, between the parallel actions of people and/or other actors over time and the underlying morphogenetic processes of the algorithm expressed in the code. The Genetic Programming and L-system example is introduced to illustrate how the text can also represent a directly symbolic approach to morphogenesis, the older Artificial Intelligence paradigm, as distinct from the Artificial Life morphogenetics of agglomeration diffusion and so on.

The standard approach is that:

> We might say 'what is a corridor?' or 'What is a village?' or 'How can we understand so and so's architecture?' So then we measure these things and, for instance, we say – a corridor is a spatial component with a measure of X.

In the unpublished dipl. Eng. thesis of Kramer and Kunze (2005) they showed that using an evolutionary algorithm, which was tested by a fitness function based on co-visibility and accessibility criteria, they could generate a wide range of spatial organisations that 'looked like' corridors, courtyards and other morphologies by setting the rules for criteria at certain values. Their professor, an architect, wanted to extend the discussion to think about why and how these things could be explained – how is it that these things 'looked like' corridors – were they really corridors or just marks on paper and so on?

In that case the discussion can lead to an infinite regress, by questioning all forms of representation, taking a phenomenological stance, invoking history and society – we can go on and on forever without nailing it down. It is just a pattern after all! So the idea here is that, in order to cut through this, we just say a corridor is a pattern you get when you set the parameters on this generative process of walls and gaps to so and so and run the code.

So a corridor is an outcome that satisfies a certain balance of global accessibility and visibility criteria which are synthesised by the generative algorithm for developing patterns of lines.

Ultimately this is an attempt to reposition the computer in architecture away from the 'look no hands, I don't know anything about programming, but I know what I like' attitude of the architectural profession to a now developing interest in getting to understand this new tool (writing as well as reading the computer, as Alan Kay said). We are trying to understand what are the implications of the new representation, what does coding do to the architectural design process.

If architects are to be systems designers, then they will need to think algorithmically, to be able to propose algorithms to a computer in order to develop their thoughts by observing the outcomes. This book proposes that, while one can do this up to a point with ready-made system exploring applications, the really creative thing is to define the algorithm using the text of an algorithmic language. The nearer we get to talking directly to the machine, the more freedom we have. The history of computer languages has been a balancing act between total freedom of programming in machine code (for really specialist needs and for those with masochistic tendencies) and higher abstractions of ever increasing ease of use, but ever more limited scope. It is unfinished work to define a really useful compromise for programming architectural systems, but it is the most interesting task ahead for computing and design.

References

Alexander, C. (1965) 'A City is not a Tree'. *Architectural Forum*, 122, No. 1.

Alexander, C. (1974) *Notes on the Synthesis of Form*. Cambridge, MA: Harvard University Press.

Anderson, S. (1966) *Problem-Solving and Problem-Worrying*. Architectural Association (private communication).

Angeline, P. J. (1994) *Genetic Programming and Emergent Intelligence*. Cambridge, MA: MIT Press.

Bertalanffy, L. von (1971) *General System Theory Foundation Development Application*. London: Allen Lane.

Boden, M. (1996) *The Philosophy of Artificial Life*. Oxford and New York: Oxford University Press.

Boden, M. (1977) *Artificial Intelligence and Natural Man*. New York : Basic Books.

Broughton, T., Tan, A. and Coates, P. S. (1997) The Use of Genetic Programming in Exploring 3D Design Worlds. In Junge, R. (ed.) *CAAD Futures*. Kluwer Academic Publishers.

Casti, J. (1992) *Reality Rules II*. John Wiley & Sons Inc.

Chomsky, N. (1957) *Syntactic Structures*. The Hague: Mouton.

Coates, P. S. (1999) *The use of Genetic Programming for Applications in the Field of Spatial Composition*. In the Proceedings of the Generative Art Conference, Milan.

Coates, P. S. and Frazer, J. (1982) *PAD Low Cost CAD for Microprocessors*. Eurographics 1982.

Coates, P. S. and Jackson, H. (1998) *Evolutionary Models of Space*. Proceedings of Eurographics UK, Leeds.

Coates, P. S. and Jackson, H. (1998) *Evolving Spatial Configurations*. Eurographics 98 ICST. London.

Coates, P. S. and Makris, D. (1999) *Genetic Programming and Spatial Morphogenesi*s. Proceedings of the AISB conference on creative evolutionary systems, Edinburgh. Society for the Study of Artificial Intelligence and Simulation of Behaviour, Sussex University, Department of Cognitive Science.

Coates, P. S, Jackson, H. and Broughton, T. (1961) Chapter 14 in Bentley, P. (ed.) *Creative Design By Computers*. San Francisco: Morgan Kaufmann publishers.

Cullen, G. (1961) *The Concise Townscape*. Architectural Press.

Dawkins, R. (1996) *Climbing Mount Improbable*. New York: Norton.

Dawkins, R. (1987) *The Evolution of Evolvability*. Artificial Life Proceedings of the Interdisciplinary Workshop on the Synthesis and Simulation of Living Systems (ALIFE '87), Los Alamos, NM, USA. pp. 201–220.

Foerster, Heinz von (1984) 'On Constructing a Reality': Lesson on Constructivism and 2nd Order Cybernetics. In *Observing Systems*. Blackburn, Virginia: Intersystems Publications.

Forester, H. and Zop, G. W. Jr (eds) (1962) *Principles of the Self-organizing System*. Pergamon Press.

Hillier, W. (1996) *Space is the Machine*. Cambridge University Press.

Hillier, W. and Hanson, J. (1982) *The Social Logic of Space*. Cambridge University Press.

Hofstadter, D. (1979) *Goedel Escher Bach*. Basic Books.

Hofstadter, D. (1995) *MetaMagical Themas*. Basic Books.

Kay, A. C. (1993) *The Early History of Smalltalk*. New Media Reader. ACM SIGPLAN Notices. Volume 28, No. 3.

Koza, J. R (1992) *Genetic Programming: On the Programming of Computers by Means of Natural Selection*. Cambridge, MA: Harvard University Press.

Lynch, K. (1960) *The Image of the City*. MIT Press.

March, L. and Steadman, P. (1971) The Geometry of Environment. Methuen.

Miranda, P. (2000) *Swarm Intelligence*. In the Proceedings of the Generative Art Conference, Milan.

Maturana, H. (1978) Biology of Language: The Epistemology of Reality. In Miller and Lenneberg, *Psychology and Biology of Language and Thought*: *Essays in Honor of Eric Lenneberg*, New York: Academic Press.

McCarthy, J. (1978) *History of Lisp*. Stanford University 1979.

Onions, C. T. *Oxford English Dictionary*. Oxford University Press.

Papert, S. (1980) *Mindstorms: Children, Computers and Powerful Ideas*. Brighton: Harvester Press.

Pask ,G. (1976) *Conversation Theory: Applications, Education and Epistemology*. Elsevier.

Pask, G. (1968) *An Approach to Cybernetics*. London: Radius Books.

Piaget, J. and Inhelder, B. (1956) *The Child's Conception of Space*. London: Humanities Press.

Resnick, M. (1994) *Turtles, Termites and Traffic Jams*. MIT.

Schroeder, M. (1991) *Fractals, Chaos, Power Laws: Minutes from an Infinite Paradise*. W. H. Freeman & Co.

Snow, C. P. (1959) *The Two Cultures and the Scientific Revolution*. Cambridge University Press.

Varanda, F. (1982) *The Art of Building in Yemen*. MIT Press.

Weiscrantz, L. and Cowley, A. (1999) *Blind Sight*. City University.

Walter, W. Gray (1951) An Imitation of Life. *Scientific American*.

Wolfram, S. (2002) *A New Kind of Science*. Champaign, IL: Wolfram Media Inc.

Index and glossary

This text is available online at:

http://uelceca.net/Index_and_glossary.htm

With the advent of Google and Wikipedia, these entries are to be seen as nudges to the start of some web searches rather than complete definitions.

AdA

The countess of Lovelace, the only child of Lord Byron who moved in mathematical circles in the mid-nineteenth century and worked with Babbage on his mechanical proto – computers (Difference engines). She is credited as being the world's first system analyst, hence her name was given to the computer language AdA, which was designed by a committee at the US Department of Defense. It never really took off.

Addresses

The memory of a computer is made up of many separate locations of memory in which to store binary data, each location has an address (literally like your house, number 0 number 1, 2, 3, 4 … etc.). Turing machines can store program and numerical data in these locations, also the addresses of other locations. This is like having an address book on your kitchen table which is at your address, but contains all your friends addresses (points to them, hence pointers (q.v)).

Agent

An Agent in computing terms is an autonomous unit of computation. A piece of code that finds and uses its own data and makes its mind up about what to do. *See* Turtles.

Agglomerative,

Clumping together in a mass. The slow development of some morphology (q.v.) by the accretive action of some process. The Alpha Syntax model and the diffusion limited aggregation models are examples.

AI (or GOFAI – good old fashioned AI) – Artificial Intelligence

The idea that computers can be programmed to think intelligently. This was intimately associated with MIT and LISP (q.v.) from the work of Newell and Simon in the 1950s. It is remarkable of the optimism of the early pioneers that only a few years after the birth of the computer designed by John von Neumann, they were already contemplating 'giant brains'.

AL – Artificial Life

Another thing this book is about, stemming from the work of the early cyberneticians (q.v.), is an approach to intelligence and problem solving based on naturally occurring methods of evolving systems of cognition and other useful behavior on the bottom-up principle (q.v.). AL gives us Genetic Algorithms, Agents, Cellular Automata, and other examples of *distributed representation*.

Alpha

As in the Alpha Syntax model of Bill Hillier (q.v.). This is a set of theoretic descriptions of spatial configurations of a very simple kind, used to represent the morphology of unplanned settlements. It was introduced, together with a range of other syntaxes, in the paper of 1978. The book contains a thorough description of this together with a program to generate such things.

Alexander, Christopher

161

Christopher Alexander wrote some seminal books on design theory from a systems perspective. *Notes on the Synthesis of Form* introduced the idea of 'natural' design as found in the development of the vernacular. His work was significant in promoting an algorithmic approach to morphology. His later work included the *pattern language,* which was an early example of a formal systems approach to design. He later repudiated the mathematical approach.

Algorithm/algorithms

1–3, 6, 9, 11, 13, 15, 21, 23, 29, 33, 38, 41, 43, 45, 47, 49, 51, 53, 56, 57, 59, 61, 63, 70, 71, 73, 80, 89, 93, 95, 97, 99, 101, 105, 108, 109, 111, 113, 115, 119, 123–127, 129–133, 137, 139, 141, 148, 151, 153, 155, 157, 159, 160, 163–168

What this book is all about. The name comes from Arabic, as does algebra, the Al prefix being the equivalent to 'the'. It is normally given as 'a set of instructions that guarantees a solution or answer to some problem'. The trouble with this is that many algorithms (often referred to as heuristics) do not formally stop, or may stop with a 'good enough' answer as in evolutionary algorithms. In this book algorithm refers to the text of some computer code, rather than any general recipe.

Allele

99

The is a little chunk of a gene (q.v.). In the genetic algorithms presented in the book, each allele usually represents one of the parameters for the development process, such as how high, how twisty, what colour, etc.

Analogue

164

Generally applied to computers to distinguish them from 'digital'. Analogue machines are built out of circuits that are 'analogous' to the systems being modelled, such as resistors, spinning disks – all the components of the elecro-mechanical world before the invention of electronics (the valve q.v.). In the widest sense it can be used amusingly to refer to 'normal' things, so an abacus is an analogue calculator, and Gaudi's gravity driven catenary models (*see* Gaudi) are analogue load distribution models. Americans spell it 'analog'.

APL

29

A Programming Language, of course. Devised in 1957 and used by IBM in the early 1960s. It had a sophisticated notation which allowed the manipulation of entire matrices of data rather than the simple variables and arrays available to most languages at the time. IBM manufactured special electric typewriters equivalent to the golf-ball typewriter to allow the matrix maths notation to be printed. It remains in use, but is something of a curiosity these days.

Archigram

123

A group of young architects mostly at the Architectural Association in the 1960s whose members included Peter Cook, Ron Herron, David Greene Mike Web and others. They published a series of small pamphlets and articles in *Architectural Design* magazine at the time, and Archigram has become an institution, recently publishing *Architecture Without Architecture*, and receiving the RIBA medal.

Ashby

124, 137

Ross Ashby was one of the British Cyberneticists who devised the law of requisite variety and built the first self-organising machines – the homeostat. A good introduction is to be found in Pickering's essay *Cybernetics and the Mangle*, where he introduces Ashby Pask and Beer.

AutoLISP

66, 77, 111

A version of LISP embedded in AutoCAD, used in many of the examples of recursion.

Autopoeticists

39

Autopoesis, or 'self-making', was introduced by the Mexican Biologist Humberto Maturana. He developed the notion of structural coupling and based his philosophy on the notion of cognition, which he saw as a natural consequence of being embodied in the world. He is popular with computer (Alife) scientists because his theories can be used to build simple feedback systems of agents and environments, where he provides an epistemology useful for understanding the models of space and cognition, a kind of bottom-up approach to intelligence.

Axioms

54, 111

Generally in logic, the set of givens or first principles that begin a proof or theorem. In the context of this book, the initial symbol string that is used to initiate a production system, illustrated using L-systems (Lindenmayer systems q.v.).

Barrio

123

An example of a squatter (unplanned settlement). In this case the name is that given in South America.

Bertalanffy

169

Karl Ludwig von Bertalanffy (b. 19 September 1901, Vienna, Austria; d. 12 June 1972, New York, USA). The originator of systems theory. His insight was to see that, although each area of science had its own special approaches, there were certain things that unified them all, the general mathematical approach to the relationships between elements of a collection of parts. As this applied to the more discursive 'nearly' sciences, like newly emerging social sciences and linguistics, it gave respectability (or spread the hegemony, if you prefer) to these new studies by being able to treat them in the same way as the 'big' boys and girls of physics.

Bilateral

111

Two-sided. In the case of morphologies it implies a symmetry about an axis. This useful attribute provides a good plan for vertebrates with balanced arms, wings, etc.

Biomorph

Dawkins' (q.v.) term for the little drawings he evolved with his program, also the name of that program.

Blind sight

80

The curious effect of being able to 'see' in the sense of somehow knowing where things are without them being displayed in the mind's eye. People whose brain has been damaged and who think themselves blind can nevertheless perform many tasks that should require vision when asked to 'guess' or trust in instinct. This suggests that there is a primitive non-reflexive facility that can drive our bodies through the world that acts as a precursor to what we think of as sight.

Boden

82

Margaret Boden, the English AI/AL academic, whose *Artificial Intelligence and Natural Man* has, for many years, been a good introduction for the rest of us. She has also written on creativity.

Body Plan

94, 95, 101, 105, 111

Dawkins introduced the Body Plan in his paper *The Evolution of Evolvability*. It is a useful notion because it shows how having a morphology that can be parameterised can lead to the fast evolution of lots of usefully shaped animals. It explains the Cambrian explosion, on the basis that once bi-lateral symmetry and segmentation had been included in the green pool it was relatively painless to churn out many types of ammonites and early worms and so on.

Bohr, Niels

13

Niels Bohr defined the characteristics of the atomic structure in terms of the quantum leap between different shells of energy levels in the atom. Used in this book as a parallel to think about the multi-ring NetLogo models in Chapter 1.

Boids

89, 91, 159

Craig Reynolds' artificial birds used to demonstrate flocking (q.v.). This became the canonical demonstration of emergence, and was part of the development of artificial life as opposed to intelligence. The simple parallel distributed algorithm (q.v.) leads from a random sprinkle of boids to a well-organised flock, demonstrating self-organisation.

Bootstrapping

3, 54, 55

The term used to describe how a computer, on being powered on, brings itself into existence (puling itself up by its own bootstraps, as we say in English). Of course Newton's laws of movement preclude this impossibility, but in an information machine it becomes more possible.

Bottom-up

21, 123, 161, 167

As opposed to top-down, the idea that you can investigate phenomena by starting from its simplest components and simulating their relationships to generate the overall structure. Part of the notion of emergence. *See* top-down.

Breeding

93, 99, 102, 108, 111, 113, 115, 119

A term borrowed from farming and botany which is used in the book in the context of Genetic Algorithms. In this case the mechanisms for combining the genes of successful individuals to make new copies of themselves.

Broadbent, Geoffrey

113

An English academic and architectural theorist. His *Design in Architecture* (1978) could be said to have been the foundation for decades of architectural theory including *A Plain Man's Guide to Semiotics*.

Bug

27, 31

The term for a bit of code that does the wrong thing. Named after a fried insect in the ENIAC at Princeton.

Buridan's Ass

84

The classical description of being in a dilemma between two equally attractive choices. Invoked by Grey Walter on observing Elmer and Elsie who seemed not to be fazed by this problem.

Chomsky, Noam

2, 3, 6, 27, 111, 113, 160

Referred in this book only as the person who defined recursive grammars formally. This led to the development of many formal grammars and production systems. See the Dom-ino house examples.

Chromosome

95, 99

A complete package of genetic material. In Generic Algorithms (in the book) individuals only have one chromosome made up of many alleles (q.v.).

Cobol

29

Common business oriented language defined at much the same time as FORTRAN in the late 1950s. Used for programming stock and payment applications, and so on.

Code

3, 7, 9, 15, 17, 21, 23, 25, 29, 33, 41, 45, 55, 57, 63, 73, 79, 85, 93, 95, 97, 101, 105, 107, 112, 113, 117, 121, 125, 131, 132, 135, 159, 167, 168

What this book is all about. Code is literature; learn to read it!

Commodore

153

One of the early 8-bit microprocessor-based computers. It used the Motorola 6502 chip as did Apple for the Apple II. The Commodore Pet is long forgotten, whereas Apple are still manufacturing machines.

Compiler

3, 77

A computer program that translates a text written in a human readable language into a machine readable form.

Complex/complexity

11, 13, 15, 29, 37, 41, 43, 47, 49, 51, 61, 68, 71, 73, 75, 83–85, 87, 93, 113, 115, 117, 119, 121, 123, 125, 129, 131, 132, 137, 165

To be distinguished from complicatedness. Complexity is the idea that a quite small collection of linked components can generate a very large number of usefully different outcomes. In particular, that the outcomes are not specified somewhere in the system, but emerge once you start the system up. This book is about complexity.

Conditional

3, 10, 31

The computer science term for asking if something is true or not and then conditionally executing some code.

Configurations

6, 23, 119, 123, 137, 139

A word for a collection of linked things in a particular pattern. The things are linked together (configured) to provide some global output.

Constructionist

26

A theory of education set out by Piaget and Papert, whereby students constructed their knowledge rather than being given the structure by the teacher. A method that has been universal in schools of architecture for 100 years.

Cybernetics

137, 159

The standard definition is theory of control in the animal and the machine. In this book invoked in the context of ideas about feedback and systems of feedback loops leading to complex behavior.

Darwin, Charles

53, 99

The Victorian philosopher and naturalist who published *The Origin of Species* in 1858 that set out the theory of evolution by competition and the survival of the fittest. This is a readable book, not too long and, in fact, possibly the first popular science book. Read it!

Dawkins, Richard

95, 101, 165, 166

Richard Dawkins wrote *The Selfish Gene* in 1977, but as far as this book is concerned presented his *Biomorph* program in the *Blind Watchmaker*. A dedicated Darwinian, his *Evolution of Evolvability* (1988) is a good text about his early evolutionary algorithms.

Debugging

27

The most important thing to learn in programming – how to find and remove bugs (q.v.). Similar to going through the strategic moves necessary to diagnose why the car does not start. Most programming environments provide tools for debugging, including variable inspection, inserting breaks and stepping through the code line by line.

Delaunay

17, 18, 19

Invented by Boris Delaunay in 1934 (Wikipedia), Delaunay triangulation is a computational geometry procedure for joining a field of dots with lines to end up with close packing triangles. *See* Voronoi.

Dijkstra

27

One of the fathers of computer science (as opposed to computer craft, which maybe is what most of us do), he was most famous for the shortest path algorithm, and being horrid about Basic. This is referred to in the book, it is mostly the one about GOTO.

Dodecahedral

109

Twelve-faced in Greek. One of the Platonic close packing solids – a shape that will fill space with no gaps. It is more interesting than the basic cube because it has four rather than three planes of symmetry, thus affording a wider range of geometries. It is used here as another way of getting round 'the everything at right angles to everything else' problem.

Dom-ino

111, 113, 115–117, 119, 121, 167

Le Corbusier's (q.v.) famous example of standardisation and production for the masses. A basic pillar slab architecture as illustrated in the context of the Genetic Programming chapter. Le Corbusier thought it was a good basic design for twentieth-century mass housing and he was not all wrong.

Dynabook

35

A graphics-based mini-computer designed by the pioneer computer designer and all round guru, Alan Kay (q.v.).

Eisenman, Peter

113

Peter Eisenman is referenced in the book because of his experimental deconstructions based on the architecture of Terragni. Subsequently he published 'diagram diaries' and also designed a range of white villas in a kind of citrohan house style as part of the New York 5.

Embryology

93, 95, 109

Given the genetics, there are a wide range of unfoldings that could take place , but as part of the genetic inheritance there is also a pattern-book for how to interpret the genes that drives the initial development into the full phenotype. When you write a Genetic Algorithm you can experiment with different embryologies to see what different body plans come out (q.v.).

Emergent

1, 9, 11, 15, 17, 21–23, 26, 39, 43, 45, 47, 49, 73, 75, 80, 83, 87, 89, 91, 111, 113, 115, 116, 119, 121, 123, 124, 129, 137, 139, 142, 143, 147, 151, 159, 164, 165, 167
Basically what this book is all about.

Epistemic

9, 123, 159, 167
With meaning – carrying some explanation of the meaning of something.

Epistemologies

123
A collection of different ways of knowing something.

Epistemologists

27
People who like to think about different ways of knowing things.

Favela

123
See Barrio.

Feedback

1, 9, 37, 43, 47, 51, 84, 93, 123, 129, 131, 137, 151,155, 160
A very fundamental aspect of cybernetics and systems thinking generally. Generally negative feedback is like the thermostat and other controllers that try to avoid systems departing from some norm, while positive feedback is like an explosion. Most complex systems have both. Maruyama (q.v.) is used in the book as an example of positive feedback.

Fitness

93, 97–99, 101, 104, 105, 110, 166, 168
In terms of Genetic Algorithms, the measure of the winning potential of an individual in an evolving population. Darwin called the driving force for the evolutionary process 'survival of the fittest'.

Flocking

88, 89
The process of producing the emergent structure of a coherent mass of birds out of an unordered set of birds. As it is best to describe a flock by its self-organising principles of a mass of birds rather than some overall geometry, it is a good exemplar of the bottom-up principle.

Foerster

123
Heinz von Foerster, one of the founders of cybernetics, referred to in this book because of his lucid exposition of the concept of open and closed systems which Maturana (q.v.) was to develop in the context of cognition and 'self-organisation'. Like Ross, Ashby and Pask, he published on homeostasis, which is a way of thinking about how systems in some relation agree to settle down into a stable state in the face of varying and chaotic inputs from their environment.

FORTRAN

21, 31, 130, 135, 136, 163
Possibly the oldest programming language in the universe, in the sense of human readable high-level code. It was devised by engineers and used by scientists, unlike LISP (q.v.) which was developed from the theories of church and post, and was defined as conceptually complete system to be used by the AI pioneers.

Frazer, John Hamilton

28, 109
Wrote a book called *Towards an Evolutionary Architecture* (1995) – very good, you should read it.

Frei, Otto

164
The engineer who developed the Stuttgart Institute for Lightweight Structures, which became a centre for the exploration of analogue computation of complex forms using soap bubbles, sand piles, etc. He is famous for the 1970 Munich Olympic stadium roof, and he also pioneered in computation models of complex surfaces .

Gaudi

164
Spanish architect who was perhaps the first generative modeller. Mark Burry of Melbourne university has spent many years developing mathematical abstractions of the ruled surfaces that seem to have been the generators of the Sagrada Familia church in Barcelona. On the other hand, his upside down models of centenary curves in 3D that developed the overall shape of the nave and aisles of the church can be considered very similar to Otto's explorations of form (q.v.).

GEB – *Gödel Escher Bach*
63
Gödel Escher Bach, Douglas Hofstadter's 1980 book on Artificial Intelligence, LISP and Kurt Gödel's incompleteness theorem. This is one of the most influential books about AI written at a time when it was still seen as an arcane and possibly bad idea. It introduced the idea of recursion (q.v.)to a wide audience. Hofstadter later took over the job of writing the mathematical diversion column from Martin Gardner in the *Scientific American*.

Gene
95–101, 109
The basic packet of information passed from one generation to the next by evolving life forms that contain the instructions to grow a new individual of the species.

Generate/generative
2, 3, 6, 9, 15, 29, 47, 68, 71, 72, 75, 77, 79, 81, 93, 105, 111, 113, 115, 119, 121, 123, 125, 137, 155, 159, 160, 164, 166, 167, 168
What this book is all about.

Genotype
95, 105–107, 111, 115, 119
The information contained in the gene, to be considered together with the phenotype, which is the actual instantiation (physical object in the world) of this information under the control of the generative process of embryology (q.v.).

Global
7, 9, 41, 43, 49, 69, 91, 123–125, 129, 136, 143, 145, 147, 151
In computer languages a variable that can be accessed from anywhere in the program as opposed to local. Also the idea that the global observer can see the overall pattern in the outcome of the bottom-up process of simulation undertaken by locally defined processes (Hey look ! It looks like a circle!).

Gödel, Kurt
63
Swiss mathematician and philosopher who was responsible for destroying Bertrand Russell and Alfred North Whitehead's *Principia Mathematica* – a late Victorian attempt to build a whole mathematics on the idea that 1 + 1 = 2. It led to all sorts of problems. See Douglas Hofstadter's *Gödel Escher Bach* (GEB) and Roger Penrose's *Shadows of the Mind*.

Goethe
29
One of Germany's finest poets and philosophers, invented the concept of morphology (q.v.).

Goldberg, David
98, 99
A student of Holland's, David Goldberg wrote a good book called *Genetic Algorithms in Search, Optimization, and Machine Learning*, which sets out in pseudocode all the algorithms necessary for building a Genetic Algorithm.

Graph
109
A graph in this context is a diagram of the connections in some system of components. The graph can be represented in a matrix form and a range of measures can be derived from it. Phillip Steadman introduced graph theoretic representations of the plan in *The Geometry of Environment* (1970) and Bill Hillier used graphs to define a range of measures to do with the Alpha Syntax formalism (q.v.).

Gray
84
See Walter.

Hillier, Bill
80, 123, 139, 160, 167
An English architectural theorist who, after a stint as the RIBA's intelligence officer, where he developed the four function model, moved to UCL where he promulgated space syntax (q.v.). The original article was published in *Environment and Planning B* in 1978, where the author's attention was drawn to a footnote to the effect that the theory was to be tested by a series of computer experiments. It turned out they had not been undertaken, so I was able to step in to the breach. See the chapter on alpha syntax (q.v.). Space syntax was a set theoretic system of recursively defined agglomeration algorithms, where well-defined expressions were unfolded by hand into morphologies covering a wide range of urban and architectural patterns of space and solids. In his subsequent books, Hillier enlarges on this to couple it with a similar description of social relations, as in the *Social Logic of Space*, though he returned to the spatial eventually with *Space is the Machine*.

Hofstadter, Douglas

62, 63

Wrote *Gödel Escher Bach* in 1978 –a very useful introduction to Artificial Intelligence, and also a good exposition to LISP and recursion (q.v.). *See* GEB.

Holland

99

Invented Genetic Algorithms – *see* Goldberg.

html

3

HyperText Markup Language – *see* hypertext.

Hypertext

3

Hypertext is a word coined by Ted Nelson (who is one of the pioneers of computing and wrote the book *Computer Lib* in the19'70s). The 'hyper' bit refers to the idea that this is better than plain old text because in hypertext each item of the text (i.e. word) has some built in intelligence, namely a link to some other bit of text. This was a revolutionary idea 40 years ago, and, after ignoring it for many years, was stolen and built into the world wide web. Ted Nelson has spent many years trying to gain recognition for his innovative idea, but by now this is like trying to patent air, it being ubiquitous and of course taken for granted.

Inductive

163, 164

Proposing that something has a good chance of being the case based on a large set of observations, as opposed to proposing that because of a statement such and such a thing must be true (deduction). Induction is relied on as a way of building theories based on multiple simulations and other computer-based methods, as set out in this book.

Instantiation

13

The act of bringing a thing to being in the world, such as generating a phenotype or any other generative process.

Isospatial

109, 110

The dodecahedral close packing array is a good example, all the nodes of such an array are the same distance from their nearest neighbour. In a cubic or rectangular array, there are two different distances – the one along the axes, and the diagonal one. In a cubit 3D ca, therefore, there are both face-joining relations (of one unit length) and also the corner to corner diagonal relations of $\sqrt{unit.2}$ length. For purists this can be seen as a bias or lack of perfect symmetry, which skews the results.

Isosurfaces

88

An isosurface is a surface developed out of all the points the same (given) distance from some other point. A sphere is an isosurface of a single point, with a set of points (such as the trajectory of an agent (q.v.)) you can get complex curved structures.

JavaScript

53, 61, 70

A programming language much used in web pages. It is loosely related to Java, which is popular because it is hardware independent, but this is something this book is not about so we will not go into that.

Koza, John

105

John R. Koza published a book on Genetic Programming in 1992 which was considered the start of the Genetic Programming craze, and certainly led to early work at CECA (we published papers on Genetic Programming and L-Stems in 1995 and 1997). It turned out that there had been some precursors (Cramer in 1985) and indeed there were reports that one of the LEO programmers had written a program to pass the 11+ exam in the 1950s. Koza introduced the idea of using function trees in LISP as the description of the genome, which became popular in the subsequent years. It is all in the book.

Le Corbusier

113, 119

Architect; only referred to in the context of the Dom-ino house.

Morphology

99, 102, 109, 113, 115, 119, 123, 129, 139, 143–147, 149, 155, 159, 163

Goethe (q.v.) is credited with inventing the word and the idea of morphology. Before that apparently people did not think that things had shapes as a property that could be abstracted and compared between things, which is hard to imagine. Remember Goethe is pronounced 'Gerter'.

Morphogenesis

160, 165–167

The birth of form – all of the models in this book are examples of this.

Mutations

99

A vital part of the evolutionary algorithm is the very small random copying mistakes that lead to hopeful new phenotypes. Included because Darwin put the development of species down to random variation under survival pressure. The mixing of parental genetic material by sexual selection is also a powerful generator of variety. Nature itself strives for a zero error copying process and in the case of cloning achieves near perfect results. This is dangerous if the environment is rapidly changing, but a low cost option worth a gamble.

NetLogo

7, 8, 11, 13, 17, 21, 40, 41, 45, 63, 84, 124, 127, 132–134, 141, 148, 164

A free programming development platform based on Logo, but with lots more turtles.

Neumann, John von

40, 41, 47, 53, 54, 56, 61, 148, 165

John Von Neumann designed the first electronic computer. He also gave his name to the von Neumann Neighbourhood (*see* Moore).

Normalising

89

Normalising a value or a vector means to redefine it in terms of the number 1. So for directions and so on it allows one to compare like with like by removing the aspect of magnitude. In the book this reference is to normalising vectors.

Nova

126, 130, 136, 137

The Data-General *Nova* was a mini-computer popular in the late 1970s for scientific research.

Occam's Razor

129

The idea that one should try to explain phenomena with the minimum of mechanisms or technical details. The usual example is that of Gallileo, whose solar-centric universe made much more sense much more simply compared with the excessive complexity and special cases of the preceding Ptolemaic system.

Parameters

2, 51, 77, 93–97, 101, 105, 115, 119, 124, 137–139, 153, 155, 165, 166, 168

A function or other kind of procedure can be supplied with values on which to work, so that by giving different values one gets different results. Parametric modelling is one where the values supplied to the model can be varied to produce different results. A piece of software with no parameters need only be run once, which is quite dull.

Parsing

2

Analysing a string to break it down into its grammatical components.

Pascal

3, 152, 153

A programming language named after the French philosopher Blaise Pascal (b. 19 June 1623; d. 19 August 1662). The Pascal programming language was devised by Niklaus Wiirth at ETH (the Zurich technical institute which was Einstein's alma mater) expressly for teaching structured programming, a way of writing code in self-checking logically related lumps or blocks. It was a way of making the structure of the code – the syntax – define the semantics in such a way that if the code passed the syntax check it could be relied on to be also logically and semantically correct as well.

Pask, Gordon

123, 124, 159

The British cybernetician (1928–96) who developed a range of theoretical approaches to education (conversation theory) and who made important contributions to cybernetics with his chemical computer and other devices that demonstrated ideas about autopoesis, ontology of machines, and new epistemologies. After many years of being ignored, his ideas are being enthusiastically taken up by a new generation of bright young things.

Pet

153

The Commodore Pet was one of the first micro-computers based on the Motorola MOS 6502 processor (as was the first Apple machine). *See* Commodore.

Phenotype

95, 96, 99, 102, 105, 109–111, 115, 116, 119

The embodiment of the genotype, what you get after running the embryology and development process to make a fully fledged individual. The phenotype is what you test with the fitness function to establish the individual's likelihood of survival.

Phototropism

84

Light-seeking behavior, often seen in plants, and used here to describe a light-sensing robot. Moths are phototropic, which is why they fly round and round candles (stupidly it turns out – an example of a (no doubt useful) evolutionary behavior which works badly in a world of human beings).

Piaget, Jean

27

Jean Piaget (1896–1980), developmental theorist and 'genetic epistemologist', who was a great influence on Seymour Papert (q.v.) in his development of LOGO.

Pixel

35, 37, 38, 55, 80

Everybody knows what a pixel is these days.

Pointers

55

In computing, a pointer is specifically a number held in memory that references an address in memory, thus the value points to another location which, in turn, contains a value. So, for instance, if you have a blue box, inside which is a message 'look in the red box', then maybe the red box has some useful information inside. So the blue box points to the red box. Some languages like C use pointers a lot, some like Basic do not. In LISP, the actual content of a symbol is a pointer, you have to 'quote' the symbol to get the value out.

Polygon

87

A many sided shape.

Polyhedra

6

A many faced solid.

Pond slime

9

A very simple pond dwelling organism used by Maruyama as the basis of a demonstration of a deviation amplifying positive feedback.

Positivists

160

An Anglo-Saxon philosophical movement that continentals are always rude about. It makes no bones about the idea that science, for instance, is the way to find out the truth about observable events, whereas of course the French in particular talk about kinds of truth. In the book, positivism is owned up to, in particular, the Chomskyan idea of deep structure – a linguistic notion of underlying order in contra-distinction to surface structure, which is adopted in some discussions of morphology of vernacular settlements.

Predicate calculus

27, 161

A formal method of obtaining proofs from sets of axioms. The language PROLOG is an example of a well-developed predicate calculus system, used by GOFAI (q.v.) people such as Winograd and is the basis of SHRDLU (q.v.).

Price, Cedric
123

English architect who represents the system's view of architecture with his projects in the 1960s where the design was to work out the kit of parts and how they went together, after which the actual building could be seen as the emergent outcome of the manifold ways they were put together.

Production
71, 72, 73, 76, 77, 111, 121, 147, 159, 160, 161, 163

A production system is a recursively defined rewrite system, which can be used to generate shapes or sentences out of any symbol string in a rule-based manner. The Lindenmayer system is such a system (q.v.) and in the book this is much discussed. Starting from an axiom the production rule is applied recursively to symbol strings where the rule is:

1. look for the thing to recognise (the left-hand side) in the string;
2. replace this with a different set of symbols (the right-hand side) to expand the production; and
3. take the new string and do it again.

See the book for many examples of this, including 'the Italian dinner', taken from Douglas Hofstadter's *Gödel Escher Bach* (q.v.).

Programming
3, 8, 10, 17, 29, 31, 33, 61, 67, 73, 83, 93, 105, 111, 113, 121, 127, 159, 163, 166–168

What this book is all about.

Pseudocode
97

An attempt to cast 'computer speak' into real normal English, but actually it remains just a way for people who talk computer speak in different languages to communicate. The best example I know of is Goldberg's book (q.v.) and mostly it is a kind of baby Pascal (q.v.).

QuickDraw
55

A series of highly optimised machine code routines for doing the graphics on the Apple Macintosh, based on the Motorola 68000 16-bit processor, including the idea of bit-blit for almost (or lets admit actually) instantaneous dragging of blocks of graphics memory across the screen (remember that until recently it was not possible to drag a Windows' window across the screen with real-time refresh. Bill Atkinson wrote the QuickDraw routines for the Apple Mac and also MAC PAINT, the original user-friendly graphics program that came free with every Mac.

Recursive
63–65, 68, 71, 77, 79, 80, 115, 127, 141

A recursive function is one that calls itself. It provides (after the initial call) its own arguments by supplying itself with its own output. To be very crude, it eats its own shit. This is a potentially endless process; so all recursive routines need a conditional statement to make sure it finally comes to an end. Recursion is a superset of iteration, or looping, but is more interesting and is often used to make self-similar fractal or branching type structures. See, in particular, the LISP section in the book.

Reductionist
1

A rude thing to say about people who think that all things can be explained by pulling them apart and cataloging the bits and pieces. It works quite well for machinery, but ignores the tendency of complex systems to have emergent outcomes that are not actually to be found in any of the parts, but rather in the relationships between the parts – which are lost when you pull it apart.

Reynolds, Craig
89

One of the founders of Artificial Life whose BOIDS is the canonical algorithm demonstrating the ideas of distributed representation and emergent structure.

Schroeder, Manfred
125

Manfred Schroeder, whose book *Fractals ,Chaos, Power Laws* is a very readable introduction to the ideas behind these things – good book.

Script

10, 23, 26

Another word for program, usually reserved for simple automation tasks and non-professional type programming. Scripting is for people who are not computer scientists, and who do not expect to be writing operating systems and massive applications for a living.

Serial

1

As opposed to parallel, the idea of doing things one at a time in some predefined order.

SHRDLU

82, 83

The language developed by Terry Winograd to build his blocks world system (explained in the book as an example of GOFAI – intelligence as logic programming). It is also the top row of letters on a linotype machine – the right hand; the left hand was ETAOIN, together the most commonly occurring letters in English. As mentioned in the book, also the name of a character in a Michael Frayn novel *The Tin Men* (1965) about an AI newspaper.

Siggraph

Special Interest Group for Graphics. An annual conference that grew out of early computer meetings where graphics was a specialised issue. The heyday was the 1970s when most of the fundamental algorithms were reported.

Smalltalk

29, 32, 33

The object oriented programming language invented by Alan Kay. Somehow it never caught on, partly because its massively recursive parallel structure made it very slow. It is still supported by enthusiasts and is generally a good thing, but . . .

Snow, C. P.

1

C. P. Snow was a scientist by education who wrote in the middle of the twentieth century about the great divide between scientists and arts graduates, bemoaning the fact that the arts graduates delighted in being innumerate, while the scientists, between doing the maths, would dutifully take an interest in Shakespeare, Bach and Rubens. Fifty years on, this is still true. Architects sometimes manage to bridge the divide, but it is still the case that it is thought impolite to take too large an interest in the technical.

Stack

66, 77

A particular way of storing data, on the FILO principle (first in last out). It is traditionally used during recursion to store the intermediate results of a recursive call, which are pushed onto the stack, to be popped out when the call ends. In the old days one would often get a stack overflow when you ran out of memory during a very deep recursion.

Stanford, Anderson

161, 164

Stanford Anderson, an architectural theorist who wrote a seminal paper in 1966 on computer-aided design, decrying the box-ticking reductionist approach which he called the justification approach – when, after a lengthy brief constructing process by the 'expert client', a building was said to be fully functional when all the aspects in the brief could be checked off. Instead he proposed problem worrying as opposed to problem solving.

StarLogo

8

The original version of NetLogo (q.v.) developed at MIT in 1995 by Michel Resnik.

Steadman, Phil

161, 166

Phil Steadman wrote *The Geometry of Environment* which remains the foundational work and introduced the notion of the graph-based representation of the plan, along with many others. He remains active in the field of representation, and has published many books. His last one is about evolutionary design in architecture.

Stiny, George

111

George Stiny who developed shape grammars. His PhD thesis was published as a book in 1973, and the study of shape grammars flourished over the next 20 years. He was never interested in computational approaches, but Ulrich Flemming, for instance, did useful work, culminating in the LOOS system for generating architectural plans. The basic principle of a shape grammar is very similar to a production system (q.v.) where there is a left hand side (thing to recognise) and a right hand side (thing to replace it with), only instead of symbols, as in an L-system, he uses diagrams of spatial units.

Structuralist

160

This is a kind of positivist approach whose heyday was the mid-twentieth century. Chomsky (q.v.) is the most relevant one here, and notions of deep structure and surface structure derive from linguistics, but are referred to in the book in the context of the vernacular architectural spatial arrangements, and also the Genetic Programming (q.v.) examples where shape grammars (q.v.) are evolved.

Sub-tree

106, 108, 109, 115, 116, 119

In any branching system, one can identify smaller trees attached to the big branches as it were. In Genetic Programming (q.v.) Koza style, these sub-trees can be gathered up and added to the library of automatically defined functions to build up the richness of the genetic material. See the dom-ino house (q.v.) experiments.

Swarm

1, 88–91, 125

The group behavior of flocking birds – *see* Reynolds.

Syntactic

2, 27, 113

Syntax is the grammar of a production, the rules that define its structure, as opposed to semantics – what it means.

Systems

1, 2, 8, 17, 26, 27, 29, 31, 35, 39, 41, 47, 51, 53, 68, 69, 71, 73, 75, 80, 81, 83, 85, 93, 95, 104, 105, 107, 109, 121, 124, 125, 129, 135, 136, 139, 140, 143, 151, 153, 155, 159, 160, 164, 165, 168

There is no one-liner about systems, best to read the book.

Tautologous

123

An argument that asserts or implies the result of what it is trying to prove – a circular argument. This is a bad thing when demonstrating emergence where the mechanisms that lead to the emergent structure must be demonstrably independent of the structure of the outcome. You cannot explain the honeycomb structure of a bees' nest by telling them to draw hexagons, instead you build some self-organising system of cylinders that press on each other to slowly make the hexagons appear. It is all too easy to fall into the trap of tautology. Even the NetLogo ant colony model is guilty of giving the ants little compasses!

Taylorism

160

The time and motion studies of the late nineteenth century that developed in the Pittsburgh steel mills and mass production generally. The aim is to break the craftsman's job down into smaller and smaller pieces, each timed and arranged in sequence so that untrained people on low wages can replicate the skilled work of the machinist. Turning people into robots essentially.

Teletype

34

A kind of automatic typewriter, often used for input (typing stuff in) and output (printing stuff out). Very often it could produce punched tape as well. Very noisy. When VDUs (visual display units) became cheaper and ubiquitous, they were originally referred to as glass teletypes.

Tessellation

9, 11, 15, 17, 45, 49

The business of tiling the plane with repeating shapes.

Thermionic

84

The thermionic valve (Americans call it a vacuum tube) was the precursor of the transistor. Used in the first computers as an on/off device (hence the valve) based on the triggering of the state change by changes in voltage.

Voronoi

11, 14–18, 45

A Voronoi diagram is a kind of tessellation based on points (2D or other dimensions) where the edges of the Voronoi cells define a minimum energy network. In 2D they approximate to a hexagonal tessellation and in 3D dodecahedral. They have many intriguing properties, defining maximum efficiency structures, but are used in the book as an example of the difference in code and approach between the bottom-up emergent approach and the top-down computational geometry approach. It is probably easier to read the passages on emergent tessellations than understand this rather clumsy attempt at a definition.

Walter, Gray W.

84, 85, 87

The American electronic engineer, then living in Bristol, who, in 1948, built the world's first two robots Elmer and Elsie. In the book, they are introduced as an example of emergent behavior, where very simple systems, coupled together, produce complex 'life-like' behaviors.

Winograd, Terry

82, 83

Terry Winograd is another foundational person, though if Grey Walter can be seen as the start of AL (q.v.), Winograd might be the end of AI. His 'blocks world' robot program is mentioned in the book – *see also* SHRDLU.

Wirth

3

See PASCAL.

Wolfram, Stephen

164

Stephen Wolfram, the programmer of Mathematica, is relevant to the book as a long time enthusiast for Cellular Automata. His 2000 tome, *A New Kind of Science*, even goes so far as to assert that the fundamental particles of the universe are computation, and that everything is a Turing machine in essence.

Image credits

The author and publisher would like to thank the following individuals and institutions for giving permission to reproduce illustrations. We have made every effort to contact copyright holders, but if any errors have been made we would be happy to correct them at a later printing.

Page 32
Extract from *The Early History of SmallTalk* by Alan Kay (1993).

Page 34
Courtesy of Rutherford Appleton Laboratory and the Science and Technology Facilities Council (STFC). www.chilton-computing.org.uk/gallery/home.htm

Page 36
Courtesy of Wikipedia. http://en.wikipedia.org/wiki/file.colossusrebuild_11.jpg

Page 56
Reprinted with permission of John Wiley & Sons Inc.

Page 62
Courtesy of Cargill Corporate Archives.

Page 66
Courtesy of xkcd.com

Page 82
Courtesy of Terry Winograd: published in *Understanding Natural Language*, Academic Press, 1972.

Page 85
Courtesy of the Burden Neurological Institute, University of Bristol, UK.

Page 86
Thanks to Jamie Tierney for the photograph.

Page 112 (top-left image)
Le Corbusier. Maison Dom-ino 1914. Plan FLC 79209. © FLC/DACS, 2009.

Page 131
Milsum, J. H. (ed.) (1968) *Positive Feedback*. Oxford: Pergamon Press Ltd.

Page 138 (bottom image)
From *Space Syntax, in Environment and Planning B*, 1976, vol. 3, pp. 147–185. Courtesy of Pion Limited, London.

Page 146 (top image)
Khudair Ali, MSc Computing and Design thesis, UEL Architecture and the Visual Arts.

Page 164
(top image)
Courtesy of Wolfram Science: www.wolfram.com
(bottom image)
Wilensky, U. (1998). *NetLogo 1D CA Elementary Model*. http://ccl.northwestern.edu/netlogo/models/ CA1Delementary. Center for connected learning and computer-based modelling, Northwestern University, Evanston, IL.